GET TECH

GET
TECH

UNDERSTAND COMPUTERS, THE INTERNET AND

CUT THROUGH THE AI HYPE

EMMANUEL MAGGIORI

Published by Applied Maths Ltd

ISBN 978-1-8383372-0-9 (print)

ISBN 978-1-8383372-1-6 (ebook)

CONTENTS

Introduction   7

PART I: COMPUTING

1	The Power and Limits of Computing	13
2	Digital Computers	27
3	Computer Programming	49
4	Hard Problems	69
5	How to Speak with Techies	75

PART II: THE INTERNET

6	The Internet	85
7	The Web	101
8	Navigating the Web	117
9	Encryption	125
10	Big Data	139
11	The Cloud	151

PART III: ARTIFICIAL INTELLIGENCE

12	Machine Learning	161
13	Predictions that Matter	177
14	Deep Learning	191
15	Beyond Supervised Learning	203
16	The Limits of Machine Learning	213
17	The Five Commandments of AI	225

Conclusion   229

Index   233

INTRODUCTION

I F you would like to understand the world of computers, this book is written for you. Perhaps you're an entrepreneur, a business manager, a recruiter, or someone who likes to know how things work.

In your job, you may have to collaborate with programmers, AI specialists and other sorts of techies, but you may find it hard to communicate with them. They keep using cryptic words and getting caught up on problems you thought were easy to solve.

Or you may be an entrepreneur with a promising start-up idea, but you're having a hard time gauging how difficult it would be to build your product, or if it is buildable at all. If this is the case, you're not alone. Over the past few years, I've been approached by countless entrepreneurs who had innovative ideas but were unsure about their technical feasibility.

For example, a few years ago, an entrepreneur had been concocting a business idea and wanted some advice on a couple of extra features he had in mind. One of them was a piece of software that would automatically analyze satellite images to predict how trees would grow in a neighborhood. It would then assess if a grown tree would block a nice view from a property and estimate the resulting drop in the property value. Thinking this was easy to do, he was considering adding it as a secondary feature in a credit risk-assessment app. Much to his chagrin, I had to tell this entrepreneur that making predictions from satellite images was a rather challenging task. This minor product feature he'd thought up turned out to be pushing the boundaries of innovation and would require a lot of work.

This kind of confusion is to be expected, since no one's born knowing how computers work. And it is often counterintuitive: What is easy for us humans to do, like identifying a person in a picture, is not as easy for computers, and what is straightforward to do with computers, like multiplying large numbers, is not easy for us.

In fact, to work with computers effectively, techies train for years and end up developing a whole new language and a new way of approaching problems. This book will help you understand both.

The first part of this book is about computing. It will help you understand the basis of how computers process tasks and how these tasks need to be expressed for a computer to process them. You will get an idea of how software developers spend their time. You will also see that some problems are much harder to solve than they seem at first glance.

But we cannot speak about computing without discussing the Internet. I'm sure you're a user of it yourself, possibly from several devices at once. And you've probably heard of IP addresses, port numbers, VPNs and encryption, but you may not know exactly what these terms mean.

If you're a tech entrepreneur, there is a high chance that whatever you're building it will have something to do with the Internet. But are you still wondering exactly what a front-end developer does or why you have to pay a fat bill to a cloud computing provider?

The second part of this book will help you understand how the Internet works and the challenges behind building Web applications. It will demystify terms that are commonly used but not always understood.

Finally, what about artificial intelligence? Everyone seems to have an opinion about it. Some people think the latest developments in AI are as revolutionary as the Internet was some time ago. You may have been told that your job is at risk due to AI. You'll soon be replaced by robots, they say. But, at the same time, you've been told for years that autonomous cars will soon be roaming the streets, yet you don't see them anywhere. How do you cut through the noise?

If you're an entrepreneur, you've probably been told you *have* to say you're doing AI—it's a magic word to gain attention from investors. I even knew a company that kept hiring AI specialists, even though their product didn't involve AI, just to claim that they were doing cutting-edge innovation. Its employees weren't very happy about that.

The third part of this book will help you understand how AI really works. You might have heard buzzwords like *deep learning* or *AlphaGo*, and here you'll see what they are really about. I'll also share with you the limitations of AI, which I've seen first-hand by working in the field. If you're thinking of using AI in your business, this will help you understand its capabilities and why some things may not turn out as you expected.

I decided to write this book after speaking with many entrepreneurs who wanted to learn about computers but thought it was too hard. The thought of computer science textbooks and online coding classes was daunting enough that it wasn't even worth a try, they said. This book is neither of those things. It seeks to help you understand the world of computers yet fit into your busy life.

Now here we go. Enjoy the ride!

PART I

COMPUTING

1

THE POWER AND LIMITS OF COMPUTING

WOULDN'T it be great if there was a toy model of a computer that could help you understand what *any* computer can do? It turns out that such a model exists and is really easy to grasp. This model is a great starting point for understanding the world of tech and the seemingly impossible complexity of computers today.

Alan Turing was a computer scientist best known for designing the device used by the Allies in World War II to crack the German secret codes. But, a few years before that, in 1936, Turing presented a famous model of a problem-solving device. This model, developed years before modern computers appeared, was not necessarily meant to be constructed as is but to help the world understand the power of computers. It is now known as the Turing machine.

Turing presented compelling evidence that his machine, practicalities aside, was capable of solving *any* computable problem. Computable problems are those that can be solved by following a limited number of steps and thus are great candidates to be processed automatically by a machine. For example, the division of two numbers is computable. In fact, you probably learned in school (and, if you are anything like me, have since forgotten) a technique to divide numbers by pen and paper. This sort of recipe, which involves a series of systematic steps, is formally known as an *algorithm*. If you can write an algorithm for a problem, then you can solve it using Turing's prototype.

This is a remarkable property because it sets the boundaries of computation: computers may come in all sorts of fancy packaging, but they can't be more capable than a Turing machine. Nearly a century later, no one has found a computable problem that cannot be solved by Turing's prototype.

As you can imagine, modern computers are a bit different from Turing machines in their implementation, but they are fundamentally equivalent: today, an algorithm is coded in a programming language, but each of the elements in the program could be implemented in a Turing machine. Now let's see how a Turing machine works; this will help you understand what a computer can do, how it does it, and why a techie needs to approach a problem in a certain way to solve it with a computer.

Assume for now that you're given a very simple task, which goes as follows: You read inputs from a QWERTY keyboard. Every time the user presses the "a" key, a light automatically turns on and stays on until a different key is pressed. For example, if you type the word "computational," the light bulb turns on (and off) twice, once for each "a."

This machine would need to store information about which *state* it is in, in order to identify whether or not it is appropriate to turn on the light. You can see this kind of "stateful" behavior all around you on a daily basis. For example, a traffic light is at a certain state at any point in time: green, yellow or red. If a traffic light didn't "know" its current state, it wouldn't be able to decide which light to turn on. In your problem, the machine would need two states: one after "a" has just been pressed (in which the light should be on) and another state after any other key has been pressed (in which the light should be off).

States by themselves are not very useful: you need a policy on how to switch between them. Traffic lights are constantly switching states in a predefined way at the tick of a clock, from green to yellow, yellow to red, and so on. Your machine would also need to define how to switch states, not at the tick of a clock but at the press of a key. Its logic is represented in the following scheme:

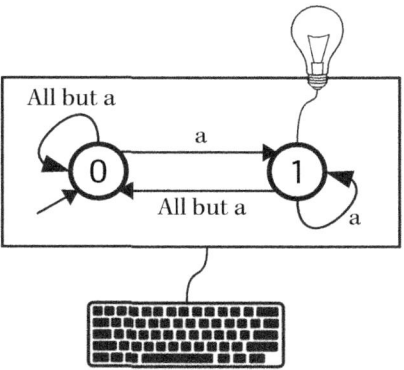

The two circles represent the states, with state zero conveying "light off" and state one "light on." The initial state (when the machine is turned on for the first time) is zero, which is indicated by the little input arrow coming from nowhere. The rest of the arrows describe the transition policy. If the input read from the keyboard is any letter but "a," the machine remains in the initial state and does nothing, which explains the loop around state zero. If the keyboard reads "a," it jumps to state one, which is connected to the light bulb and turns the light on. As long as the key pressed keeps being "a," it stays in that state, as indicated by the other loop, but otherwise it goes back to zero where it started.

Let's ignore the details of constructing this machine for now. I'll ask you to believe me that it wouldn't be too hard to build this machine since it's pretty much a glorified traffic light.

You may be thinking that this framework is fairly limited. However, let me show you how it can perform more complicated tasks. Let's say you want a machine to turn on the light only right after the user types the word "hey." The machine to do this would be set up as follows:

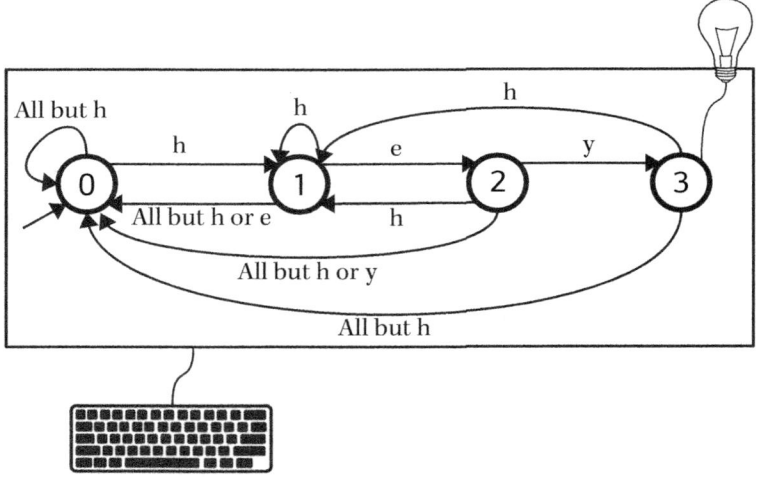

Note that if you type "hey" the path leads straight forward to the light bulb, but any other keystrokes send you back to intermediate states or to the beginning.

Let me show you another example before moving on to the real Turing machine. Let's say you want to turn on the light after the word "hey" is typed an even number of times, but other words may be entered in between without affecting the count. That machine would look like this:

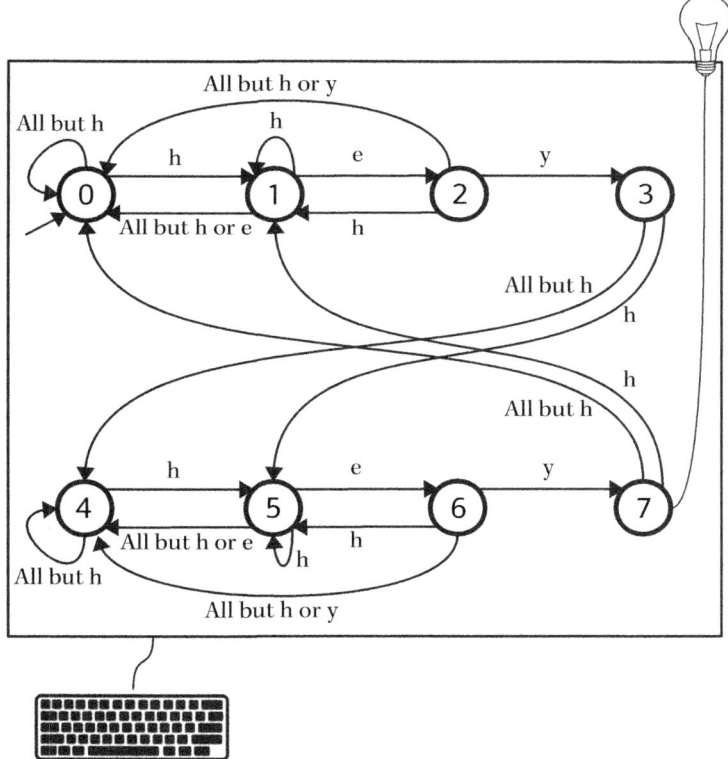

As you can see, things start to get bigger, but you can still perform the task using the same simple framework. In fact, you could design a machine that does the same thing with one fewer state. If you're feeling curious today, you could try to sketch that smaller but equivalent machine.

In my first year of university, one of the courses involved designing machines like this on paper to perform a multitude of tasks. In the beginning, some tasks seemed impossible to achieve with only this limited set of tools, but, with some training, we would end up finding creative ways of doing it. For example, we designed machines capable of counting things and performing basic arithmetic. You'd often design a very complex configuration only to find that a classmate had managed to solve the same problem using half the number of states. These sorts of design problems helped us train our brains to think computationally: after all, this is how computers operate.

While states and transitions can take you further than you'd expect, they still can't solve any computable problem because they can't record things and go back to them later. Because of that, the Turing machine has an additional component: a tape. This adds the last needed ingredient to solve any computable problem: a memory. A complete Turing machine looks like this:

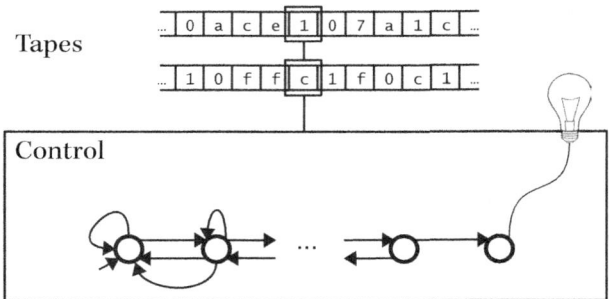

One tape is enough, but you can add more for convenience, as in the figure above. A head, like you would find in an old audio cassette player, is used to read and write from the tape. A Turing machine can read the user input from one of the tapes, so I removed the keyboard in this model. Since there are no keystrokes, the machine is governed by a clock. At every tick, the machine reads an input from the tape and switches to the next state as configured in its transitions. In addition to just jumping states, a transition can instruct the machine to write a character on the tape as well as to forward or rewind it. This allows it to store and retrieve intermediate calculations for later use, as you do when you multiply numbers or solve puzzles by pen and paper.

With this added capability, you could get creative and configure a Turing machine to convert Fahrenheit degrees to Celsius, for example. The user would first write the required input on a tape before starting the machine (e.g., "32.0° F"). The machine then executes the series of steps necessary to first subtract 32 from the input and then divide it by 1.8, which is the algorithm to convert Fahrenheit to Celsius. Some serious number crunching is involved in the process, jumping around several states at every tick of the clock and using auxiliary tapes to store intermediate results. The final answer is written into another tape ("0.0° C") and the light is turned on to indicate that the calculation is finished. I will spare you the details of this configuration, which would most likely span the rest of this chapter, but I'd like you to believe me that it can be done.

In fact, as I've said before, this machine can be configured to solve *any* computable problem. The algorithm that detects your face in a Facebook photo could be executed by a Turing machine. The machine would read from a series of numbers (an image is a table of numbers where the color of each pixel is given by a number) and then it would perform a series of operations described through the set of states and transitions, such as finding if certain patterns are present in the pixel values. It would output the coordinates of the bounding box around your face by writing them to an output tape and turn on the light to indicate that the process is complete.

The moral of the story is, however simple a Turing machine may seem, it establishes what a computing device can do, which is solve any problem whose steps can be laid out in an algorithm. The computers of our daily lives are a bit different: they have a

RAM instead of a tape and a disk for long-term storage, they send signals to other machines through a cable under the ocean, and they read inputs from interactive sources such as a mouse. These features are for interactivity, convenience and speed, but they are not adding more computing capabilities to the old Turing machines. The latest advances have added computing power, not capabilities. Even the most sophisticated artificial intelligence software follows the instructions of an algorithm religiously, just as a Turing machine does.

Now consider the case of randomness. How would you generate a random number with a Turing machine? These should be unpredictable, yet Turing machines follow a list of predefined instructions, which is as predictable as it gets. The answer is very simple: it is not possible.

When I was a (geeky) teenager, I remember playing with the built-in random number generator of a programming language. Throughout the execution of the program, I used the generator to repeatedly output numbers, which looked something like this: "7, 4, 23, 9, -8..." The sequence certainly looked random to my eyes. However, every time I reran the program from scratch, I would see the exact same sequence, "7, 4, 23, 9, -8..." It turns out that the apparent randomness generated by computer programs works by taking an initial number, known as the seed, and performing a calculation on it to obtain the next one. The new number is then used as a seed to generate the following one, and so on. The operations performed at each step are quite obscure, such as taking the remainder of a division and shuffling digits around. The results look pretty random. However, if you know the starting seed and the algorithm, then the rest of the sequence is completely predictable.

If you plan to open an online poker room, you are in big trouble since the players could potentially predict how the cards are dealt. Luckily, lots of creative solutions to this problem have been implemented and are readily available to programmers. For instance, you could set the initial seed to the time at which the game started, to the millisecond, combined with some information from the server's operating system, which players are not authorized to see, such as how much memory is being used in the system at that moment. Alternatively, you could use a device to generate truly random numbers from a physical process. For example, the website random.org has been around for over twenty years, capturing atmospheric noise from a radio receiver to generate random numbers for its users. You could also buy a 50-dollar USB device that looks like a memory stick, which measures a chaotic electrical process to provide you with a constant flow of truly random numbers.

All this is to say that computers follow a recipe to the letter. This is also true of the most sophisticated artificial intelligence algorithms, such as those that recognize objects in images. For example, consider a program that determines whether or not there is a cat in a given picture. The state-of-the-art algorithms for this problem apply a vast series of filters, which are mathematical operations intended to highlight a specific aspect of an image, such as lines or corners. A set of filters could be designed to detect whiskers by highlighting clusters of dark lines, which would provide compelling evidence that there is a cat in the picture.

It would be quite a painful process for a person to define every detail of this program by hand. For example, do we need a filter for whiskers? If we do, what are all the possible shapes and sizes of whiskers? The modern approach uses another program to define those details, rather than doing it manually. This second program systematically scans thousands of images of cats, looking for patterns to determine the most useful filters to detect "catness." The information gathered from this is then used to configure the specifics of another program. This is known as *machine learning*, a type of artificial intelligence that will be discussed later in this book. It may seem magical at first, but the program that decides if there is a cat in the picture and the one used to configure its filters both follow a fixed sequence of steps that could be implemented in a Turing machine.

Once you have designed a Turing machine to perform a task (its states, transitions and tape operations), you could build a dedicated physical machine that implements the intended behavior. That's how traffic lights are built—they only perform the intended task and nothing else. But that is impractical because you would need to build a different physical machine for every task.

The more flexible alternative is to build a *programmable* machine. This type of machine isn't hardwired to execute just one task. Instead, it contains physical components to perform generic operations that can be combined to perform many different tasks. The machine is given as input a program, which is a list of instructions used to tell the machine exactly what to do. Then the machine executes the required actions. That's how most modern computers work, as we'll discuss in the next chapter.

KNOW THE LIMITS

We've seen that a Turing machine can perform any task laid out as a list of steps, an algorithm. But no one said that finding that list of steps was easy! In fact, one of the great challenges of software development is coming up with the right algorithm to solve a problem. And if you don't have much experience doing that, you may have a hard time guessing how difficult it is. For example, you may have thought you could hire a freelancer on a tight deadline for a certain task but then find out that what you want to do requires months of innovative research.

I recently took a call from an entrepreneur who was working on her travel start-up and needed some advice. In the midst of the Coronavirus pandemic, she wanted to add to her website a list of travel restrictions by country. She asked me how she could use artificial intelligence to do that.

I explained to her that there was no need for fancy artificial intelligence. She could manually go through official sources, such as embassy websites, and compile her findings in an Excel spreadsheet. If any part of that process became too annoying to do by hand, it could be automated with simple tools. She said she didn't know much about tech, and that made even little tasks like this seem daunting.

More often, it goes the other way around. When I was a kid, my dad worked as a video editor. This was back in South America, where teenage girls celebrate their fifteenth birthdays with extravagant parties, akin to American sweet sixteens. They often make video skits to play for their friends on a big screen during the ceremony.

There was one girl who had what she thought was a simple request: she wanted to edit one of Madonna's music videos so that the singer would be replaced by herself in the clip. My dad and his colleagues had to explain to her that to do this would actually be a really hard task: she'd have to dance just like Madonna, to the pixel, in order to replace her in the clip in any realistic way, or she'd have to shoot the whole thing from scratch. The girl thought that some "photoshopping" could replace one person in a video with another, when what she actually needed was a magic wand or a Hollywood-style production (but on a teenager's budget). The end solution was to interleave scenes from the music video with clips of herself dancing on a somewhat similar background. At fifteen, this girl started her career in not understanding the bounds of tech. Rumor has it that she now works at a start-up incubator in Silicon Valley.

Jokes aside, overestimating the limits of computation is an easy mistake to make and is quite common among business people and even techies themselves. Let me show you a method to easily gauge the difficulty of a problem in two steps.

First, analyze the input of your problem. If it comes from a physical signal, such as a photograph, a video, an audio recording or a 3D scan, there are high chances that the problem is hard.

Suppose you want to write a program that detects moving objects in CCTV footage. It may sound trivial since all you need to do is compare the images at several points in time to see if there is any difference between them. Easy, right? Believe it or not, this problem is so difficult that it's a research field in itself. A camera always captures minor fluctuations in the signal. For example, a white wall is never a plain white wall all the time: the pixel values move slightly up and down due to clouds moving and light bulbs flickering. In fact, if you stare at a white wall yourself, you'll also notice some flickering, but as a human, you're used to ignoring it. The appearance of objects (not to mention their shadows) also changes as the day goes by and the sun sets, even if nothing has physically moved on the picture. As a result, finding the differences between two subsequent images is a poor way of detecting moving objects.

Moreover, you're not interested in all kinds of motion. For example, trees are constantly shaking due to wind, but you're interested in detecting burglars or cars, not leaves. Humans are very flexible when it comes to interpreting signals. You understand that an apple is an apple, even if its shade of red is slightly different from that of any other apple you've seen before. You also constantly ignore aspects of a signal that are not interesting, such as minor flickering, without even realizing it. But an algorithm only exhibits the flexibility that was explicitly implemented in it.

My first suggestion is thus to automatically classify a problem as hard work if it involves analyzing physical signals.

My second tip to evaluate the difficulty of a problem is to think of how many sheets of paper you'd need to write down a list of steps to solve it. For example, finding the average price of a stock over the past six months is a task that can easily be broken down into a short list of steps. You don't have to write the list to visualize its length. But say the task was to translate a document. It is really hard to come up with a definite list of steps to do accurate translation. You could easily use a dictionary to translate words one by one, but to produce a good translation you need to understand grammar, the meaning of sentences, and know what "sounds good" in the target language. If I gave you an entire notebook to write down the list of rules to translate English to French, you would run out of space. Even a hundred notebooks wouldn't be enough. This is again a sign that the problem is hard to solve with a computer, if it is solvable at all.

2

DIGITAL COMPUTERS

INSTEAD of being made of gears, cranks and levers, modern computers are digital electronic devices. But what does that even mean? In this chapter, we'll explore how modern computers work. We'll talk about their hardware components and the roles they play in allowing computers to perform the computational tasks we've seen. You've probably heard of some of these components before, like memory or CPU, but if you're like many people out there, you might not understand exactly how each piece works. For example, did you think that a laptop with an eight-core processor is twice as fast as one with four cores or that computers will keep getting faster and faster in the future? In this chapter, I'll debunk some of these myths and show you how hardware manufacturers have come up with innovative solutions to improve their products. And if you thought that the best-selling device in history was the iPhone 7, or the toilet, I have another surprise in store for you.

ELECTRONICS

Modern computers are sophisticated electrical circuits, intricate yet tiny mazes of interconnected wires. Depending on how the circuit is configured, electricity may or may not flow through different parts of it at different times. Think of the lights in your house: some of them may be on while others are off, based on how you configure the wall switches. Some of them may even be grouped to turn on or off all together.

In a similar fashion, the water pipes in your house form a sophisticated network, full of valves and junctions. When someone else is taking a shower in the bathroom and you open the kitchen tap, the person in the shower senses the reduction of water pressure. In fact, you could use this as a communication mechanism. You could send messages to the person in the shower (while also being really annoying) by intermittently opening and closing the kitchen tap. This creates a world of new possibilities: the measurements of water pressure along the pipes may be used to convey information and pass messages.

Similarly, turning switches on and off in an electric circuit has the effect of altering the electric pressure along the wires. Electric pressure is necessary for electric current to flow and is (loosely) analogous to water pressure through pipes. Electric pressure, which is measured in volts and more commonly known as voltage, can be cleverly used to convey information in electric circuits. Any device that uses electricity, such as a lamp, is said to be electrical. But an *electronic* device, like a computer, uses electricity in a more advanced way: to transmit and process information encoded in voltage values.

GOING DIGITAL

If you were to send a message from the kitchen to the person in the shower by altering the water pressure, you'd want it to be easy to understand. But, for the person in the shower, having to discriminate between many levels of water pressure would be a difficult task. You'd probably end up using something like Morse code. You would encode each letter as a sequence of short and long water pulses, which are easy to tell apart. For example, the letter "a" in Morse is conveyed by a short pulse followed by a long one (· —). In fact, the distress signal SOS became popular because it is very recognizable in Morse (· · · — — — · · ·). It is not an acronym for "save our ship" or anything like that.

The same is true in electronics: it is hard to distinguish different voltage nuances at a fine level, such as 5 volts from 5.1, and 5.1 from 5.2. Even the slightest interference from the outside world could affect the readings. Therefore, the safest solution is to only consider two voltages far away from each other so they are easily distinguishable. Typical values used are (around) 5 volts and (around) 0 volts. These two levels are known as "1" and "0."

Using just the two digits 1 and 0 to represent information, instead of a myriad of values, is what makes a circuit *digital* (as opposed to analog). Everything in the digital world is represented through a *binary signal*, which is nothing more than a sequence of ones and zeros. When it comes to numbers, this isn't hard to do, because every number in our familiar decimal system has a corresponding binary representation. For example, "5" in decimal is "101" in binary. All mathematical operations, such as adding and subtracting, have an equivalent one in binary. But when it comes to other types of information, such as images or text, everyone has to agree on how to represent it with binary digits. For example, images are represented as tables of numbers that correspond to colors in an agreed way. So when you see a "5" on your screen, its underlying representation is actually "101" inside your computer's circuitry, and the computer also has to come up with a binary way of telling the screen how to draw out the shape of a 5. For example, "Use color 100101 for the pixel in position 111011."

Each letter in a text is also given a binary number, as in Morse code. This mapping is known as character encoding. Have you ever opened a text file only to see a bunch of incomprehensible characters? This happened because the text reader couldn't identify the encoding of the text and thus had trouble translating the binary number into the intended characters.

Sometimes, there are individual wires for each of the digits of a binary number. Have you ever opened an old computer and seen a cable like this?

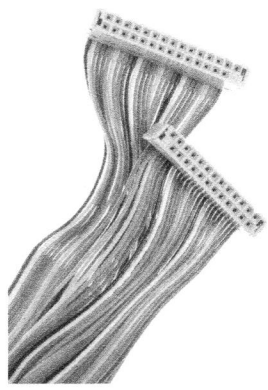

Each of the individual wires communicates a digit, 1 or 0, by means of a voltage level, high or low.

TRANSISTORS

Last we saw, you were standing in your kitchen turning the tap on and off to send Morse code messages to your friend in the shower. But you wouldn't want to have a person manually turn switches on and off in a digital circuit to encode information and perform calculations with it. That would give you a switchboard operator instead of the automatic computing device we're going for. So what do you do?

Enter the transistor.

The transistor is the most mass-produced device ever. Its

most popular variant has been manufactured thirteen thousand billion billion times. Some consider it to be the most important invention of the 20ᵗʰ century. You probably have millions in your house: inside your smartphone, your laptop, even your digital watch.

Transistors are the switches used in digital circuits, akin to valves in water pipes:

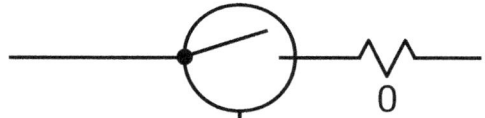

Let's assume that the wire in this drawing is part of a larger circuit, connected on both ends to a battery, and thus electricity could potentially flow through it. The jagged line on the right is a resistance, meant to slow down electricity, and an ideal place to measure voltage. It's akin to clenching your fist around a hose to gauge the water pressure flowing through it. But in this circuit, if you were to measure the voltage around the resistance, you'd get 0 volts because the transistor, represented by the circle, has interrupted the flow of electricity. Therefore, the information encoded at this part of the circuit is the binary digit 0.

The transistor has an additional input, called the gate, used to activate it. If you connect the gate to a high voltage (a 1), then the transistor switches its state and lets the current flow:

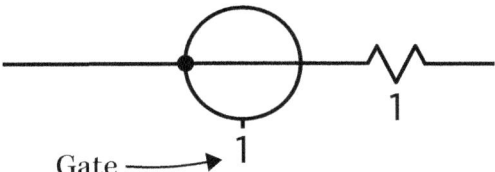

Now the voltage measured at the resistance is high, and thus the information conveyed is the binary digit 1.

Note that instead of having a person crank a lever, a transistor uses a voltage value, connected to its gate, to open or close the flow. That is, electric pressure itself is used to move the switch. This is akin to having a stream of water hit a valve and move its lever, opening the water flow in another pipe, without a person operating the lever.

In real transistors, there is no physical switch as in the drawing. The inside of the transistor is made of a material with special chemical properties, known as a semi-conductor. When the gate receives a high voltage, a 1, the material is conductive of electricity, letting the current flow through the wire. Conversely, when the gate receives a low voltage, a 0, the material loses its conductivity, impeding electric flow. The effect is similar to a switch physically moving to break the current, but the change in conductivity is a property of the material itself. Only a few very special materials have the desirable property of being semi-conductors. I'm pretty sure you've heard the name of the most common of these materials, *silicon,* after which Silicon Valley is named.

PERFORMING CALCULATIONS

Transistors can be combined, for instance by connecting the output of one transistor to the gate of another one. When done carefully, this makes it possible to use a circuit to perform calculations. Let me show you an example.

Suppose you put two transistors in a row, as follows:

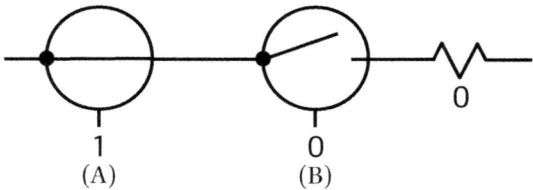

In this circuit, the output is 1 only if both A and B are 1.

Believe it or not, this is already an example of a tiny computing machine. It performs the "and" operation: the digit measured at the resistance is 1 only if both A *and* B are 1, but it is 0 otherwise.

If you put two transistors in separate parallel paths, you build a machine that computes the *or* operation because it produces 1 if either A *or* B (or both) is 1:

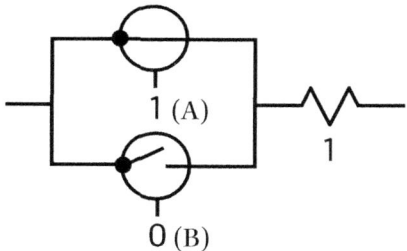

In this circuit, the output is 1 if either A or B is one.

Another useful operation is "xor" (exclusive *or*), which returns 1 if the inputs are different (one being 1, the other one 0) or returns 0 if the inputs are the same (both 1 or both 0). I will spare you the details of implementing the *xor* circuit, but it isn't much more complicated than the other two.

These units are known as *logic gates* and are often represented by the following icons instead of describing the whole internal circuitry:

And   Or   Xor

Ignoring the internal details lets you focus your attention on how to combine the components in smart ways and not on how they're built inside their little black boxes. This kind of abstraction, which makes work easier, is omnipresent in the world of tech.

The basic logic gates are important because, in the binary world, arithmetic can be done by combining them. For example, let's say you want to add two numbers, A and B, of a length of two binary digits each. Computing 2 + 3, which is 10 + 11 in binary, should give 5, which is 101 in binary. I will show you a circuit that accomplishes this task by combining *and, or* and *xor* gates. This might look a bit scary, but I don't expect you to spend time analyzing it. The point is to appreciate that logic gates can indeed be combined to do more complicated things:

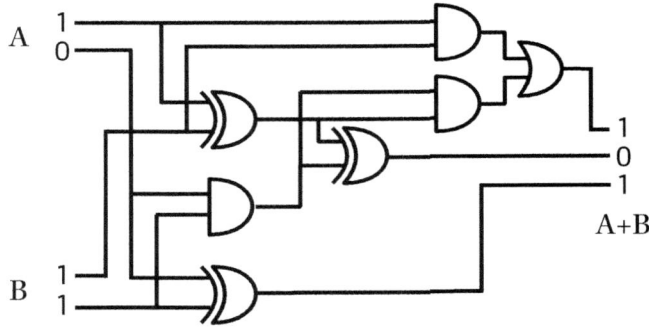

This layout outputs the correct sum for any combination of input numbers in A and B (so long as they are 2 binary digits long) and thus constitutes an effective "digital adding machine." A larger circuit can be designed in a similar fashion to accommodate inputs with more than two digits. Multipliers, comparators, and a myriad of other components are created by following similar processes. Once a component is designed, you can imagine that its contents are encapsulated into a black box for others to use:

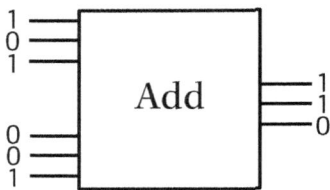

The resulting black boxes are then combined into larger boxes to solve more complex problems, and so on. Wires and transistors are combined into logic gates, and these are then combined into components, and so on, at increasing levels of abstraction, to perform more and more complex tasks. This is how digital computers are conceptually designed. In practice, the circuitry of a modern computer, often containing over 100 million logic gates with many transistors in each, is imprinted on a microscopic scale into thin sheets of silicon.

CPU AND MEMORY

We've seen how calculations are performed in digital circuits. But how are these circuits organized in a modern computer, like your laptop or smartphone?

The central processing unit of a computer, or CPU, is the main entity in charge of executing tasks and performing calculations. When a laptop comes with a sticker that says something like "Intel Core i7" it is indicating the type of CPU that comes with it. A CPU contains circuitry to perform a number of standard operations, usually at least a few hundred. You can think of it as a collection of black boxes, including adders, multipliers, comparators, dedicated units to deal with fractional numbers, and more:

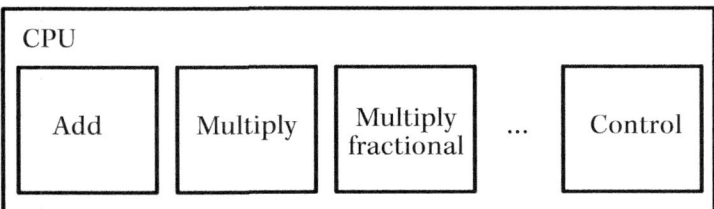

There is also a control unit that analyzes user requests and configures the rest of the modules to do exactly what is needed.

For example, if the user requests to multiply two numbers, the control unit will make sure that the relevant numbers make it to the multiplier and the output goes to the right place, while discarding the result from irrelevant units like the adder or comparator. All of this, of course, inside a microchip less than a square inch in size. Your laptop, desktop computer, smartphone and tablet all contain a CPU.

If you remember Turing machines, they use a tape to store the information needed throughout the lifetime of a program. In modern computers, this is achieved through different kinds of *memory*. The CPU is constantly reading things stored in memory and writing data to it. CPUs have a tiny memory inside their inner circuitry, known as a *register*, which is very fast to write on and read from. However, since it's expensive to produce, it is usually very limited in capacity. For example, modern Intel CPUs have 16 registers. Imagine how limited a CPU would be if it could only store 16 things at once. Due to their scarcity, registers are typically only used to store simple, immediately-needed data.

The random-access memory, or RAM, is external to the CPU and is the main memory source in a modern computer. It holds most of the data needed throughout the life of a program. For example, when you load an Excel spreadsheet, the content of each cell is loaded into the RAM, so that you can browse it and modify it in a fast way. This is also true for the various tabs on your Web browser or an image you're editing on Photoshop. The larger the RAM the easier it is to open multiple programs at the same time without facing performance issues.

Some applications are not very memory-hungry. For example, text is lightweight because every character is represented by a relatively short number. You could load the entire *Harry Potter* series in the RAM of any modern computer and still have a lot of spare room. But, in other cases, the memory requirements are surprisingly high. For example, uncompressed video (which is video that hasn't been simplified to make the file size smaller) is a succession of at least twenty images per second of video, each containing millions of pixels with color information. And that is heavy. In a computer with 16 GiB of memory (with space for over 100 billion binary digits), you would only be able to load around two minutes of high-definition video. For this reason, video editing software needs to process video in chunks because it can't load a whole video at once into the RAM.

The RAM is organized as a series of cells, each of them able to store a binary number of eight digits, known as a byte. Whenever the CPU needs to read from or write to the RAM, it indicates the location of the cell of interest by its index number. For example, the CPU says, "I want to store number 10010 in cell 10," or, "I want to read the content of cell 11."

At the physical level, cell index numbers are communicated as binary numbers from the CPU to the RAM through a set of parallel wires, one for each digit. In older CPUs, known as 32-bit, there were 32 wires capable of communicating index numbers up to 32 digits, which was quite limiting. The new standard is to use 64 digits instead, allowing many more unique addresses and thus larger RAMs.

A remarkable property of a RAM is that it takes roughly the same amount of time to read or write from any address. This is very different from disks or tapes, where you may need to spin or rewind significantly, depending on how far the desired location is from the reading head. That's why the R in RAM stands for random: not because you access things at random but because, if you did, it would take a similar amount of time.

Contemporary RAMs are fast but ephemeral; the data stored is lost when you power-off. This is why most computers come with a so-called secondary memory, such as a hard drive. Every time you "save" an Excel spreadsheet, the updated contents go from RAM to disk, so that they persist even if you turn the computer off or there is a blackout. Why not always use persistent memory then? The reality is that the current technology for persistent memory is tens, if not hundreds of times slower than the RAM and tends to force you to read or write large chunks of data in one go, even when you don't have to. Therefore, an ephemeral RAM is still the go-to technology for fast and "random" access.

However, as CPUs became faster, it didn't take long for memory access to become a bottleneck. CPU manufacturers have worked hard to improve the performance of memory access. They observed that quite often a program requests to read the same portion of the memory again and again. Therefore, they added intermediate layers between the RAM and the CPU, known as a *cache*, which "remember" a few of the results most frequently retrieved from the RAM. When a program requests a value from the RAM, the cache returns it right away if it has remembered it, which is a lot faster than retrieving it from the RAM. Adding a small cache improves performance without driving up the monetary costs significantly, with the more economical RAM still being used as the main source of memory. Making hardware perform better is not always about building faster and more expensive components: it also involves a lot of creativity.

THE PROGRAM

Executable programs are one of the most important outputs that software developers generate through their work. A program is a file containing a list of instructions that tell the CPU what to do, one step at a time. Take, for example, the case of a file ending in ".exe" in Microsoft Windows, which contains a list of steps for the CPU to execute. When you double-click on an ".exe" file, the instructions are first loaded into the RAM. This is another function of the RAM: in addition to storing any data required by the program, it is in charge of storing the program itself while it is running. The CPU then reads the instructions from the RAM, one by one, and executes each of the indicated actions using the relevant hardware components, such as the add or multiply boxes that we saw before.

Instructions are, unsurprisingly, a sequence of binary digits. The first few digits are used to tell the CPU what operation to do. For example, in the case of Intel x86 CPUs, instruction number "00000000" orders the CPU to do a sum. The next few numbers in the instruction give more details about the required operation, such as which numbers to sum or where to get them and where to store the result. A full instruction looks something like this:

$$\text{ADD} \quad\quad 5 \quad\quad \text{R1} \quad\quad \text{R2}$$
$$\text{00000000} \quad 0101 \quad 0001 \quad 0010$$

This tells the CPU to add 5 to whatever is stored in register number 1 and to write the result in register number 2. At the bottom of the instruction, I included the actual binary number, as read by the CPU. Note that everyone needs to agree on how to encode this. Imagine what would happen if programmers thought that "00000000" corresponded to multiplications while CPU manufacturers used it for sums. To avoid having to deal directly with binary numbers, which can feel unnatural and make the process error-prone, programmers use a friendlier notation known as an *assembler language*, with words like "ADD," which I wrote in the top line of the instruction. This makes things more readable when designing a program. Every keyword in the assembler language has a direct mapping to a binary number—but, of course, it is the binary version that is ultimately used in the real program. The assembler language is a rudimentary programming language that makes work a bit easier. We'll see later on how programming and programming languages have evolved.

Another common type of instruction is the following, used to "move" data:

MOVE   15   154235

This tells the CPU to write number "15" to the RAM at position 154235. This instruction has a corresponding binary number, which I have omitted, used in the real program and understood by the CPU. Note the parallel between this kind of instruction and writing and reading from the tape in a Turing machine.

Another type of instruction is the *jump*. Imagine if a program were just a linear list of instructions that went from beginning to end. You wouldn't be able to perform different actions based on the interaction with the user or depending on a previous result since you'd be obliged to always follow the same list of steps. In order to offer a more flexible execution flow, CPUs provide instructions that let you jump to another part of the program if a condition is met:

JUMP IF ZERO   10

This instruction tells the CPU to skip ten instructions, but only if the result of the previous calculation was exactly zero. You are also allowed to jump backward to a previous point in the program, possibly performing the same action again and again in a loop until a certain condition is met. This functionality can be related to the programmed transitions of a Turing machine, which define which state to jump to given a condition.

With these elements, you can write any program you want. On Intel CPUs, for example, there are around 1,500 different possible instructions, but impressive programs can be written using only a handful of them.

INTERACTING WITH THE OUTSIDE WORLD

Any useful application will obviously need to interact with the user at some point. This is done through external devices such as a keyboard or touchscreen. In any modern computer, from your laptop to your smartphone, the CPU is designed to interact with other components, not just the RAM. There are a number of input/output ports that are used to connect external devices. Among the instructions understood by a CPU there are a few to read and write data from those ports, which lets a program interact with external devices. These instructions are used to read the input from the user, such as taps on a touchscreen, and also produce useful outputs, like playing audio through the speakers. These main components—the CPU, memory, ports, and the communication channels between them—are usually bundled together in a single panel, known as the *motherboard.*

While the CPU is the main processing unit, it may delegate some tasks to other specialized secondary processors. For example, serious gamers usually connect an external graphics card, which contains its own processor especially designed to rapidly manipulate graphics and thus flawlessly render state-of-the-art 3D games. Dedicated graphics cards are also used to perform intensive mathematical calculations, such as simulating the aerodynamics of an airplane, and have become quite popular in artificial intelligence.

A COORDINATED EFFORT

If you and your colleagues have ever tried to independently edit a single Word document at the same time, you'll know what I'm talking about. Even with sophisticated change tracking tools, sometimes it's just best if you let your colleagues finish their edits first before making your own changes. Otherwise you end up getting in the way of one another's work and making a mess.

In a similar way, the execution of instructions in a processor would get really chaotic if actions weren't coordinated in time. For example, imagine that one instruction stores a number in a specific place, followed by another instruction that reads and uses the value stored there. This is extremely common since the reason to store things is that they are needed sometime soon. How can you make sure that the new value has been properly stored before the next instruction tries to read it? This isn't trivial because nothing happens immediately in digital circuits. Even the simplest instructions, such as "ADD," need some time to yield stable outputs throughout the circuitry.

To make sure that everything is properly synchronized, a digital clock is used to coordinate the processor. The clock is a wire that runs across the different components of the CPU, alternating high and low voltages in time:

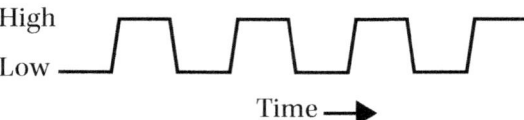

Many of the individual components of the CPU are designed to make changes to their status only at the ticks of the clock: when it goes from low to high or from high to low. For example, a register may store data during the "upward" tick and output data on the "downward" tock, thus avoiding inconsistencies between reads and writes. As illustrated in the figure above, the clock spends most of the time in either the high or low state and only a tiny fraction of the time switching between them. The long plateau between the ticks and tocks gives enough time for all the components in the CPU to produce stable outputs, and the ticks and tocks synchronize the different operations.

CPU manufacturers specify a number of gigahertz (pronounced gig-uh-hurts) or GHz for their products. This is the number of times the clock ticks per second. For example, 3 GHz corresponds to three billion ticks per second. The higher this frequency the faster the CPU clock. Some CPUs speed up the frequency dynamically when the need arises and thus quote a range of clock frequencies rather than a single value. For example, an Intel Core i7 operates in the 2.9 GHz to 4.2 GHz range.

SPEEDING UP

Does it seem to you that computers are only getting faster and faster and that the trend will go on forever? Throughout the decades, CPUs have indeed become faster and faster in terms of clock frequency, going from as low as 10 ticks a second (or 10 hertz) to billions of ticks per second (in the gigahertz). However, the process has stagnated since the early 2000s, with progress coming at a much slower rate. The reason for this, and the bane of a hardware developer's existence, is *heat*. At this point, a faster clock would literally melt the device.

However, this hasn't stopped hardware designers in their quest for better performance. Not even a little bit. As early as the 1980s, they observed that most instructions follow a similar pattern: read something, do some arithmetic with it, then store the result somewhere else. This often consumed a few clock ticks to coordinate all the efforts. But what if, at the same time you're storing the final result of one instruction, you start processing the beginning of the next one? This improvement is known as instruction-level parallelism and is a standard practice in modern CPUs. This is one creative way to speed things up without increasing the clock rate.

But overlapping instructions in this way needs to be handled with a lot of care: you cannot start processing an instruction that depends on the result of a previous one if the first operation hasn't finished yet. This results in a gap because the CPU needs to wait until the first result is available. But the gaps are filled with other instructions from later on in the program, which do not have dangerous dependencies on the result that is being waited for. And so a program is hardly ever processed just one instruction at a time or processing them in order.

This is to say that a lot of the improvements in CPUs stem from remarkable creativity and not necessarily higher speed. Nowadays, comparing two CPUs by their clock rates is not as meaningful as it used to be.

GOING PARALLEL

With the clock speed plateauing and the benefits of instructions-level parallelism saturating, we soon hit a performance ceiling again. Therefore, the next step hardware designers took was to introduce multiple "copies" of a processing unit, known as *cores*, instead of having a single one. Even smartphones nowadays have multi-core CPUs. Since these units are more or less independent, they are capable of processing separate lists of instructions at the same time, *in parallel*.

There is a significant challenge though: having separate cores is only useful when the program performs tasks that can be processed separately. For example, a Web browser can process each tab on a different core. However, if a program is sequential by nature—for instance, a solution needs to be progressively updated until reaching a goal—then it cannot benefit from multiple cores as easily.

As of today, only the programmer can decide whether a task can be split into parallel subtasks or not since this is problem-specific. Even if the task can be split, this doesn't happen automatically: the developer needs to explicitly write "subprograms" and indicate that they should be sent to different cores. Therefore, it is a misconception to think that any program will run faster just by having a device with multiple cores. This is the case only if the software developers have designed it to be that way.

When a single program is split into parts that can run in parallel, sometimes significant efforts are needed to coordinate the tasks. For example, the program would have to know to wait until all the separate units are finished and then combine the results into a final output. The overhead caused by the logistics may offset the benefits of parallelism in the first place. Going parallel is a great proposition, but it usually exhibits diminishing returns.

Over the past few years, parallelism has been extended even beyond individual computers. Large problems are split and distributed along a cluster of many computers connected to each other through a network, such as the Internet. This lets you increase the number of simultaneous tasks beyond the number of cores in a single machine. For example, using ten machines with eight cores each gives you a total of eighty processing units.

If you wanted to find a word in billions of documents, for example, you could distribute the documents across many computers and have each of them try to find the word within its own set of documents. This would to be faster than processing all the documents on a single machine. This paradigm pays off most with really large problems that involve processing a lot of data. But once again, orchestrating the different machines and sending data through the network are costly tasks, which may offset the benefits of parallelism. We'll further discuss this new model of computing in the chapter about big data.

This kind of sophisticated processing is no longer reserved just for huge companies either. Since the cloud computing revolution, which we will also discuss later on, even the smallest company can rent this kind of powerful infrastructure from an external provider and get access to enormous processing power without having to buy anything. Now anyone can play like a giant.

THE ROLE OF THE OPERATING SYSTEM

If you've ever noticed that using a Mac is not quite the same as using a Windows PC, you've experienced the difference an operating system can make. You might even have strong feelings about it. A lot of people (especially techies) swear by their preferred choice and are uncomfortable if they have to switch. But the role of the *operating system* (OS) goes well beyond the cosmetic aspects of user interfaces; they are sophisticated pieces of software in charge of managing the resources of a computer.

For example, one of their responsibilities is to enable multitasking. When using your computer or smartphone, you get the impression that many things are happening at the same time. You are allowed to open several programs at once or even watch two different YouTube videos simultaneously, if for whatever reason that floats your boat. When you program an alarm on your phone, it goes off at the right time even if you're using another app. You're not required to stare at the clock until your alarm rings.

I've just told you that modern CPUs have multiple cores and thus can physically do things simultaneously. However, that is only a recent addition. It doesn't explain how you could use multiple programs simultaneously in the times of Windows 95, when your CPU had just one core. Even if you have a multi-core CPU, it probably contains no more than four cores, but you can still do more than four things at once. How can that be?

The reality is that multitasking is quite often just an illusion. The instructions of different programs are sliced and interleaved, giving the impression that they happen at the same time.

This effect is achieved thanks to the intervention of the OS. The CPU has a built-in timer that, every few milliseconds, directs it to abandon the normal flow of the current program and run instead the instructions stored in a special memory location, which contains OS functionality. This is also triggered by other events, such as when the user presses a key.

These interruptions are used by the OS to maintain and administer the resources of the computer before resuming the normal workflow. Following the interruption, if the OS deems it necessary, it resumes the execution of a different program than the one interrupted. This is done back and forth, allocating short slices of time to each program and interleaving them, creating the illusion of multitasking. The slot assignments follow a sophisticated policy, trying to allocate more time to the hungriest programs but making sure that none of them hogs the CPU. In practice, as many as a hundred program switches take place every second.

Multitasking is just one of the many responsibilities of the OS. It also handles the interaction with external devices and manages the memory and the access to hard drives. Each operating system has its own strategies to manage resources with its own set of pros and cons.

The most common operating systems on mobile devices are iOS and Android, the latter being based on Linux.

For desktop computers, Windows and macOS dominate the consumer market because they are focused on providing a friendly user experience and a lot of popular applications are built for them.

But what about the computers that work behind the scenes, such as the servers that power the Web? For these, Linux is almost entirely the operating system of choice. Linux is open-source and comes in hundreds of different variants, known as distributions, such as Ubuntu, Fedora and Debian. Among other traits, they are highly customizable and free of charge, which makes them very attractive operating systems. They may not be the friendliest to use, but their flexibility outweighs that for many techies needing to run reliable Web applications.

Most techies you know are probably familiar with Linux concepts and know how to run commands on their black-and-white terminals. macOS is much closer to Linux than it is to Windows since they are both based on a similar older OS. This means that a techie used to working with Web servers will find working on a Mac more comfortable the rest of the time. Files are organized in similar ways, and they can run the exact same commands in both environments. This is one of the reasons why so many software developers prefer Macs.

THE FUTURE

It is hard to tell what the future of hardware holds, but one thing is clear: the current trend is to gain power by doing multiple things at the same time, rather than doing them faster. This doesn't come without its own set of challenges. It is only possible to speed up the parts of a program that can be split into independent tasks and run simultaneously. Even then, the overhead involved in doing so may not pay off. If your business needs to speed up a program and you thought buying a better computer would suffice, you may be disappointed.

We've seen that creativity is often what's needed in the quest for ever-increasing speed. The idea of an alternative model of computation, known as quantum computing, has been around for decades. It builds upon physical properties of tiny particles, rather than digital circuits, effectively escaping the binary world of ones and zeros. Despite many research efforts, it doesn't seem like there will be any "quantum" leaps in computing any time soon, but time and creative innovation will tell.

3

COMPUTER PROGRAMMING

Imagine how sad the life of a programmer would be if it involved constantly writing instructions such as "Add 5 to what's in position 17 of the memory, and save it in position 18"—and this, of course, in binary. This wouldn't leave programmers with enough free time to play *Dungeons and Dragons*, watch *Star Wars* and read manga, which are of course our favorite activities.

Jokes aside, the add-and-move kind of instructions are referred to as *low level* because they have a low level of abstraction. They are really close to the physical aspects of the machine and very far from the way in which we, humans, like to work. But this is not how programming is done anymore.

Throughout the years, computer programming has become more and more abstract: someone first creates a program to deal with low-level tasks and then other programmers use it as a set of building blocks to create higher-level applications. In this paradigm, the programmers, also known as software developers or coders, focus on the added value of their own applications without worrying too much about the menial tasks that happen under the hood. The process has become increasingly friendly with time: I have seen physicists and accountants write programs on a daily basis without knowing much about computer science.

But while it's possible to piece together some workable code without an in-depth knowledge of computer science, knowing even the basics of how a computer is programmed will help you understand what's really going on. This chapter explains just that. You'll learn how coders spend their time when they are writing software. You'll see the problems they face, the choices they have to make and what makes good quality software.

THE PROGRAMMING LANGUAGE

Let's suppose you asked a contemporary software developer to create a program to convert miles to feet. The program should read the user input from the keyboard and then show the result of the conversion on the screen. Let's assume it uses an old-school black-and-white terminal without any fancy visual interface.

Programmers write their software in vanilla text files, which can be opened on any text editor. Some use dedicated editors, with cues and shortcuts specific to programming, but the same can be achieved with something as simple as Notepad.

The following is an example of the text that implements a miles-to-feet converter:

```
variable length_in_miles = read_number
variable length_in_feet = length_in_miles*5280
print length_in_feet
```

Each line in this file is an instruction to perform a required task, but they don't look anything like the low-level instructions understood by the CPU. This code is easily readable and includes words in English. These three lines of code do exactly the three things that are needed: read a number, multiply it by 5,280 (which is how many feet there are in one mile, apparently), and then show the output on the screen.

The first line starts by declaring a *variable* with the name "length_in_miles." Variables are places in memory identified by friendly names rather than by low-level numeric locations. This makes it much easier to manage the content stored in memory because you identify things by name instead of having to remember meaningless numbers. In the same line, the "=" sign is used to store something inside that location. In this case, the keyword "read_number" indicates that the content to be stored should be read from the user's keyboard.

The following line uses the symbol "*" to perform the multiplication of the content previously stored in "length_in_miles" by 5,280 and stores the result in a new variable called "length_in_feet."

Finally, the statement "print" is used to display the content of this new variable on the screen, completing the task. For some historical reason, most programming languages have a pre-built functionality called "print" to show things on the screen, even though no printers are involved.

When coding a program, the developer needs to follow the conventions of the programming language. All of the available programming languages (C++, Java, Scala, etc.) are somewhat different from one another, each with its own pros, cons and caveats. The piece of code I showed you above follows the conventions of a fictional language that I just invented, but it is quite similar to code written in the Scala and Python programming languages. Some languages are a bit fussier than this. They might require you to explicitly indicate which type of data is meant to be stored in each variable (for example, "integer" or "character"). Others even ask you to finish every line of code with a semicolon. Small differences aside, this is the gist of how instructions are written in a programming language.

COMPILATION

The code above is not very useful by itself: as a text file, it can be edited and shared among different programmers in your organization but not executed on a CPU. That would require low-level binary instructions, known as *machine code*, instead of friendly text.

Once programmers are finished writing their text code, they use another program, known as a *compiler*, to translate it into machine code. For every line of code in the input text file, the compiler outputs the required binary CPU instructions to accomplish the task. A single line in the original code may result in many CPU instructions, depending on the complexity of the task. The result is an executable file, such as an ".exe" file in Windows, which you can double-click to run. This file is no longer easy to read but provides a low-level execution plan for the CPU to do the exact same thing intended in the original code. The overall process is summarized as follows:

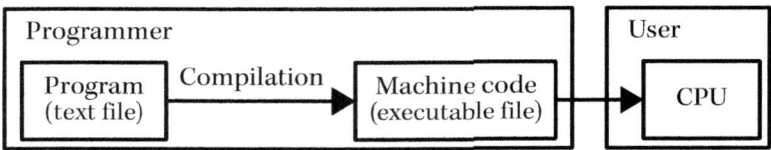

The compiler is a computer program written by someone else before, distributed as a black box for others to use. Each programming language comes with a set of standard compilers, which can be installed in any computer and are free to use. For example, if you download a C++ compiler to your laptop, you'll be able to write code in the C++ language and translate it into the corresponding executable machine code.

There is an important caveat: the resulting machine code needs be in the exact format understood by the CPU that will run it. If a programmer compiles code for one type of CPU, where the sum instruction is encoded as "0000," but then tries to execute it on a different machine, where "0000" is a multiplication, things will not work as expected. To avoid these kinds of problems, some of the largest CPU manufacturers, including Intel and AMD, have agreed on a common set of instructions. However, each of them implements them differently, and the optimal combination of instructions on an Intel processor may not be the highest-performing choice on an AMD. As a result, in order to run a program efficiently, you need to compile the code several times for different target processors and make sure to deliver the right executable file to each end user. For example, the eloquently named "AMD Optimizing C/C++ Compiler" is a compiler of the C and C++ languages that, unsurprisingly, produces machine code specifically optimized for processors manufactured by AMD. Intel also has its own C++ compiler, specifically designed to produce instructions for its own processors.

The nightmare doesn't end there: the compiled code often makes use of utilities of the intended operating system (for example, Windows or macOS). This means that a program needs to be compiled not just for a specific CPU type but also for a specific operating system. You end up with executable files for "Windows on Intel," "Mac on Intel," "Mac on AMD," and so on. You may have noticed this when downloading software, where you are offered a list of variants and you need to choose the one that matches the characteristics of your computer. One of the great advantages of the compilation process is that the resulting program is optimized to run on your physical computer set-up. However, this is also its curse because the same program now needs to be compiled multiple ways for different users.

There is an alternative paradigm that overcomes this problem: *interpreted* programming languages. In this model, the text files created by the programmers are directly distributed to users without any compilation whatsoever. If you receive one of these text files, you can open it with a text editor and look into its content. If you want to run the code, you need to open it with a special program known as an interpreter. This program reads the text file line by line and, in real time, compiles the code for your specific CPU and runs it:

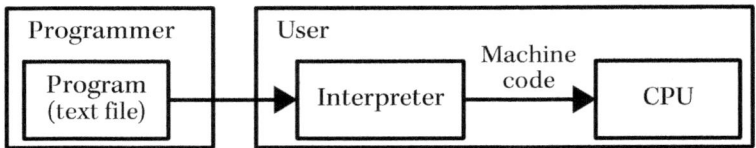

An example of this model is the Python programming language. Let's say I write this on a text file, and send it to you:

print 2+3

If you open it on a text editor, such as Notepad or Word, you will just see the code I've written: "print 2+3." However, if you download a Python interpreter and use it to open the file instead, you will now see "5." This is because the interpreter parsed that line of code and derived the necessary CPU instructions to do the required task. The interpreter translates the code into instructions that are especially adapted to the target machine and operating system.

While, at first glance, this looks much friendlier than the compiled paradigm, it doesn't come without its own set of disadvantages. For example, now the software developer assumes that the end user will have the relevant interpreter installed in their machine and know how to use it to run the code. Moreover, translating text into CPU instructions on the fly is slower than running binary code directly. Since both models have their own downfalls and perks, both are routinely used by programmers all over the world.

There is still another hybrid alternative used by one of the most popular programming languages, Java:

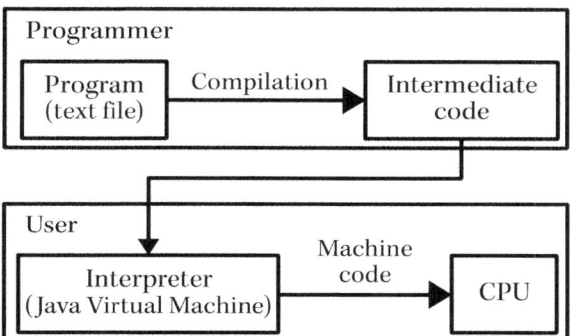

With Java, the programmer still needs to compile the code. However, the compilation does not go as far as producing CPU-level instructions. The compiler takes the original text and produces a more compact and optimized version of it. This is no longer human-friendly but still remains independent of the characteristics of the end user's computer. This intermediate code is distributed to the clients, who run it by using an interpreter they have installed known as the Java Virtual Machine. This interpreter performs the last bit of translation required to turn the intermediate code into machine code specifically tailored to the computer on which it is run. No wonder the slogan used to promote Java in 1995 was "Write once, run anywhere." Since it gets the best of both worlds, compilation and interpretation, Java has become one of the most popular languages.

CONTROL

The computer programs you interact with on a daily basis are rarely completely linear; rather, they are interactive and let you choose the course of action. When you work on an Excel spreadsheet, for example, you can choose which cell to edit. If you're scrolling through your Instagram feed you can choose to go up or down. Unless your business is building something really simple, I bet the program won't be linear.

Programming languages come with a handful of *control* statements to break the linear flow of the program. For example, "ifs" are used to selectively run code based on a condition:

```
if password_entered = "Mr. Fluffers":
    print "You are now logged in."
else:
    print "Wrong credentials. Try again."
```

The above code evaluates a password entered before by the user, stored in a variable called "password_entered." If it is equal to "Mr. Fluffers," the name of the user's Pomeranian, then it accepts the password and indicates the success with a message on the screen. Otherwise, an alternative message is shown to indicate the failure to log in. Only one of the two messages is ever shown; the message that is not shown is simply skipped over in the code. If you remember the last chapter, there are instructions that tell the CPU to skip instructions. When a compiler translates an "if," it outputs the necessary CPU instructions that jump over the irrelevant branch.

Have you ever snooped into a programmer's screen? You may have noticed that some lines of code are indented, as in the example above, leaving a blank space on the left of the text. This is a visual cue to help identify which pieces of code don't follow a normal linear flow.

Programs also often need to perform an action over and over again. For example, when you're scrolling through Twitter, you see thousands of tweets rendered in a similar way. Does this mean that a coder copy-pasted the same code thousands of times? Certainly not.

For this kind of functionality, programmers use a control statement known as a *loop* or "for." Have a look at the following example, which shows a million numbered tweets on the screen with just two lines of code:

```
for number in range 1 to 1000000:
    print "This is tweet " + number
```

This code outputs "This is tweet 1," "This is tweet 2," and so on. The code translates pretty well to plain English: "For every number in the range 1 to 1,000,000, show the message *This is tweet* followed by the number." You would probably want to do something more sophisticated than printing "This is tweet 1," like fetching an interesting tweet from a database, but you get the point.

The compiler has different ways of converting this into machine code. One is to "unroll" the loop and output a linear program with millions of CPU instructions that "print" one tweet after another. An alternative is to only include the relevant instructions once and use jump instructions to go back and run the same thing again and again until a stopping condition is met. While this second option is the more likely one, the compiler will choose the one that is most optimal for the target CPU.

FUNCTIONS

Suppose your company is building accounting software with an entire team of developers working on it. The application deals with amounts in both dollars and euros. Snippets of code are scattered all over the program to convert currencies when needed, as in the following example:

```
value_in_euros*1.14
```

This multiplies the content of the variable "value_in_euros" by an exchange rate of 1.14 to convert the value to dollars. As the code grows to millions of lines, the operation "*1.14" starts to appear thousands of times.

Repeating code like this is a terrible idea for two reasons. First, it is wordy, maybe not in the case of multiplying by 1.14, since it is a very simple operation, but imagine you needed to sort numbers several times in your code; writing the entire algorithm to sort numbers every time you need it would be really verbose. The second problem is that if you ever needed to modify the functionality, the coders would have to change it every time it appeared in the code. For example, if the exchange rate went from 1.14 to 1.15, they would have to scan millions of lines in the program and replace every occurrence of 1.14 with 1.15. It may not sound like a daunting task, but this can go horribly wrong when the program is split into multiple files and each programmer is working on a different version of it.

Wouldn't it be much easier to write the functionality just once, in a single place, and then use it as much as you need to elsewhere? That brings us to the next level of abstraction in the world of programming: writing a *function* just once and naming it for future use. For example, the following statement defines the process of converting euros to dollars:

```
function convert_to_dollars(input):
    input*1.14
```

It translates to plain English quite easily: "The functionality called convert_to_dollars takes an input and multiplies it by 1.14." This statement doesn't convert a currency by itself; it only defines how to do it when needed. Programmers can then use this functionality any time they want by *calling* it by its name and indicating the input in parentheses:

```
print convert_to_dollars(120)
print convert_to_dollars(150)
```

This toy program would first output "136.8," the result of converting 120 euros to dollars, and then "171," the result of converting 150 euros to dollars, when the exchange rate is 1.14.

If the exchange rate were to change, there is now only one place where the code that needs to be modified. The function could even be rewritten to fetch the current exchange rate from the Internet, rather than "hard coding" it into the program.

Writing functions also facilitates a stronger division of labor: every developer owns a piece of code and is responsible for maintaining it. When one piece of code is modified, others don't need to do anything about it because the names of key functions would stay the same. Splitting code into independent modules is the key strategy behind developing scalable and maintainable software.

OBJECTS

Suppose a programmer is writing an animated computer game to play basketball. Data about the ten players has to be stored simultaneously in memory to render their 3-D characters on the screen and play the game.

On the one hand, these players are all very similar in terms of functionality. They can all jump, run left and right, move forward and backward. They are also rendered similarly, as human-like figures wearing shorts and T-shirts, and they all bear a name, belong to a team and are on the court during the game. On the other hand, they are each different in terms of their individual data. Each player is in a different location on the court, has a different name and belongs to one of two teams.

How do you reconcile the fact that players are all similar to one another yet different from one another? The code to achieve this can get messy quite easily if not organized well. The programmer could easily get lost in coding all these details and end up repeating snippets of code several times.

This is when a sophisticated paradigm, called object-oriented programming (OOP), comes to the rescue. Under OOP, coders write *classes*, which are general blueprints of what an object, such as a player, looks like. The following is a simplistic example of a class that represents a player:

```
class Player:
        variable location
        variable team
        function render:
                print location
```

This class definition describes both the data and functions associated with a player. It states that a player has two representative variables, "location" and "team." It also provides a function, "render," to show the player on the screen. This class definition doesn't execute any code by itself; it is just a blueprint of a player. In a real game, there would be many more variables and functions, such as those to make players jump and move.

Programmers can then create individual players under the Player class, which assigns them all the features and functions of that class to make working with them easier later on:

```
variable player1 = new Player
variable player2 = new Player
```

In this example, the programmer created two new players, "player1" and "player2," each an object of the Player class. A full basketball game would require creating and manipulating ten objects of the Player class, one for each player on the court. All players contain their own individual data, such as name and location, but the programmer can manipulate them all in similar ways using the set of functions defined in the class. For example:

player2.render

This line of code asks the second player to render itself on the screen. Note that there is no need to write the same function several times for different players, and the coder doesn't lose track of which data belongs to which player. OOP makes it more manageable to write, organize, and manipulate many objects in complex applications like this one.

But this is just the tip of the iceberg of what can be done with OOP. It provides many ways of manipulating small pieces of code with big effects. For example, by adding a couple of keywords in the code, a class can "inherit" the behavior of another class. For example, the Player class could inherit from a more general person class, which provides generic ways to render human figures on the screen. In the Player class, the coder would then only define the things that make a player special compared to other kinds of persons. For example, players wear jerseys with their team colors. This way, it is easy to borrow existing code and build on it to suit new needs.

You could do without this paradigm in a simple application, but OOP is now the model of choice in any consequential piece of software. Finding the right object-oriented solution to a problem can be hard, and software developers spend significant efforts thinking about how to organize their classes. But their efforts tend to pay off very well and significantly improve the reusability, scalability and maintainability of code.

LIBRARIES AND FRAMEWORKS

We saw that programmers often write a function just once and then invoke it several times in a program. This can be extended beyond the scope of the program for which a function was invented. Functions can be packaged into a *library* and shared with the rest of your organization, or even the world. In general, a library contains a collection of functions to solve problems in a specific domain, such as image editing. Other programmers may incorporate the functionality of a library into their own applications, instead of coding everything from scratch.

Suppose you want to write a program to resize an image to 400 × 400 pixels. I know you can do that on Photoshop, but if you wanted to automate the process, for example, to resize thousands of images automatically, you may have to write your own program for that. Manipulating images is quite a daunting task. For starters, just opening an image file can be quite tricky. Image files are compressed using a sophisticated mathematical technique. The algorithm to undo the compression, which is what image viewers do, would probably take at least a few hundred lines of code.

But with libraries, there's no need for that. Let me show you a (real) piece of code, written in the Python language, that resizes an image file stored in the disk ("my_image.jpg") to 400 × 400 pixels and saves the output in a new JPEG file ("my_smaller_image.jpg"):

```
from PIL import Image
my_image = Image.open("my_image.jpg")
my_smaller_image = my_image.resize((400,400))
my_smaller_image.save("my_smaller_image.jpg")
```

You don't have to understand or even read this code in detail, but there are a few things I'd like you to note. First of all, it only has four lines, not thousands. Second, the first line of code imports functionality from an external library called PIL (Python Imaging Library). This assumes that the library is somewhere present and reachable in the machine where this code is being executed, otherwise the software will crash. Finally, off-the-shelf functions from the library, such as "open," "resize" and "save," are used in the code. Under the hood, the seemingly straightforward "open" function runs the algorithm to decompress a JPEG image, spanning hundreds of lines, as written by the creators of the Python Imaging Library. All you had to do was write one word: "open." The "resize" function is also quite sophisticated, even interpolating the gaps if the image size is increased from the original. But you don't have to worry about any of this since you can simply use what others have created before.

Believe me, there is a library for everything. Many of them are open source, and thus free to use, including the imaging library above. If you wanted to analyze text, you could use an external library for Python known as NLTK. If you wanted to play with machine learning, Scikit-learn does exactly that. If you wanted to add graphical elements like buttons and scrollbars to your app's user interface, you'd have a handful of libraries to choose from.

Another way of reusing other people's code is through a *framework*. As opposed to libraries, a framework controls the entire flow of the application itself, letting you "fill in the blanks" to meet your needs. An example of a framework is Django, which is used to create sophisticated websites. It controls all the interactions between users and your website, possibly adding layers of authentication and security, and lets you design your own personalized webpages while respecting the principles of the framework.

CONTAINERS

To make use of a library requires that you have a copy of it; otherwise the program cannot run the external pieces of code needed.

You usually don't have to worry about this because consumer applications like Microsoft Word generally come with an installer that sets everything up for you. It would be really annoying to ask a user of Word to get other pieces of software to be able to use it. But even so, on rare occasions, library problems do come up in mainstream software. (If you've ever gotten a "missing dll" error in Windows, it was because the program could not find a required library in the system.)

On the other hand, for many behind-the-scenes applications, such as the computer programs used to store your bank account details, to fulfill your online shopping order, to schedule your flight and track your delayed baggage, it is common to distribute a piece of software separately from its required libraries. This has always been the cause of serious headaches.

For example, if the programmer uses one version of a library and the client has another, incompatible version of it, it could cause unexpected errors or crashes. It could also happen that the program cannot find the library in the system because it assumes it is stored in one place but it is somewhere else. Things can also get out of hand quite easily if two programs in a computer require different versions of the same library. Once, my boss received a piece of code that ran properly in my computer but crashed in hers. We spent hours trying to find the problem until we figured out that one of the libraries in her computer was too old for the program to run. However, she couldn't simply replace the library with a newer version of it because that made other programs in her computer crash.

A possible solution to all this is to always ship a program together with any external libraries it uses. But this is often wasteful: when sending an updated version of your software to your client, why would you also send a new copy of every external library when none of them have changed?

An improved solution involves a higher level of abstraction and has become extremely popular over the past few years: the *container*. In a containerized application, the programmer writes a standardized configuration file, which explicitly describes absolutely everything about the environment in which the application should run, including libraries and any other settings. The software is then distributed together with that blueprint of its environment.

The application is then run by using a container manager. This tool first analyzes the requirements and automatically downloads the missing items from the Internet (or the organization's private repository). Afterward, it runs the program in a micro world inside the computer, isolated from the rest. The application inside the container is not allowed to access anything from the host computer that it is not granted, and two containers running at the same time are not allowed to interfere with each other. This guarantees that applications run exactly as expected without altering the existing libraries in a system or colliding with other running applications. Containers have made it possible to guarantee that the same software will run the same way on different machines.

Containers have also improved the scalability of software: since you can easily run your code on another computer, it is easy to hire computing infrastructure from someone else when you need additional processing power (more on this in the chapter about the cloud).

Containers take the top podium spot for abstraction in software development at the moment. Docker, the most popular container technology, has grown steadily over the past few years and will likely continue to do so.

QUALITY SOFTWARE

Learning a programming language isn't very hard. Remembering the syntax, such as where to put a semicolon, becomes second nature quite quickly. Put in moderate effort and you will soon be able to write a program that does what you need. However, simply getting the job done is not a good gauge of success in the world of software; more important is what comes afterward. A quick-and-dirty solution may work at first, but your program may be really hard to modify when changes are needed or the scope of the application grows.

That is why software must be *designed*, preferably before the first line of code is written, with the goal of organizing it in a way that is sustainable and stands the test of time. A good design structures the program to easily accommodate change, encourage the reuse of code, and work in different environments. But you don't want to "over-engineer" the solution either, making it so future-proof that it loses sight of the task at hand. It is a delicate balance.

Some changes are considered in the design and thus easy to make, while others require the coders to thoroughly *refactor* the code, which means to restructure it hoping that it will still hold together. Before you ask a software developer to make a change, I recommend you try to see which sort of work it requires. If you often ask for functionality that requires heavy refactoring but doesn't add value to the business, the developers may start not to like you very much. I once worked in an organization where it took half a day of coding and recompiling to change the price of a product, due to the reliance on a legacy system we couldn't get rid of. An upper manager kept asking to change prices, sometimes on a daily basis, without a justifiable business reason for doing so. One price change took so long to code and compile that the team member in charge of those changes didn't have time for anything else. The manager simply wasn't aware of how difficult the task was. He assumed it was a simple thing, since any properly designed system would easily accommodate a price change. But everyone was afraid to tell him.

Writing software is a collaborative process, not just inside an organization but at a global scale. A piece of software reuses the software created by someone else before, which also builds upon someone else's previous efforts. This goes all the way down to CPU-level instructions. Before writing code from scratch, it is wise to wonder if someone else has already done the same thing before. If so, it may be possible to just use it instead of reinventing the wheel. In fact, the level of abstraction has increased so much that sometimes coding is not needed at all: you can write a blog with WordPress or launch an online store with Shopify, and there you've created a useful website without ever writing a single line of code.

4

HARD PROBLEMS

Do you remember the old days of GPSs, when a soothing voice said, "Recalculating," every time you drove off the recommended path? In a couple of seconds, an algorithm found a new fastest route to your destination. But this problem is harder than it seems.

Techies spend a lot of time trying to come up with algorithms that get the job done *efficiently*, not just get it done. Let's see what this is all about.

Suppose you're given the task of designing a GPS "recalculating" algorithm. The input is a map of the city, with its roads and intersections, and you must find the fastest route from A to B:

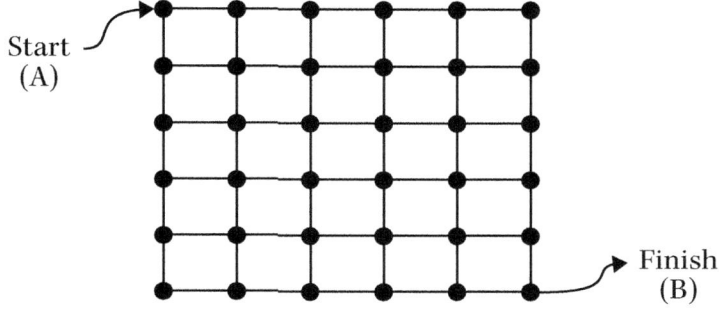

In this simplified example, the possible intersections are laid out on a grid and the path starts at the top left corner and finishes at the bottom right corner. If you zoom in, each segment is labeled with an estimation of the travel time in minutes:

The travel time may not be directly proportional to the distance, due to speed limits and traffic conditions. Let's simplify the problem even further and assume you may only take steps downward and forward through the grid, thus always bringing you closer to B.

Since you skipped algorithm design class, you come up with the following solution:

1.   List all possible paths from A to B.

2.   Compute the total travel time for each.

3.   Select the fastest path.

You code this in your favorite programming language, which proves quite easy to do.

You test your initial solution on a toy example, with a 3 × 3 grid, and it works like a charm. You move on to a 10 × 10 grid and things start to get a bit clunky. When you test it on a map of Manhattan, with a grid of size 12 × 150, you wait and wait but the program never finishes running.

Let's have a look at how many possible paths exist depending on grid size to estimate how long it would take to run the program. Assuming that you can process 1,000 paths per second, the resulting numbers look as in the following table:

Grid size	Number of paths	Total program run time
3×3	6	6 milliseconds
5×5	70	70 milliseconds
10×10	48,620	48.62 seconds
15×15	40,116,600	11 hours
20×20	35 billion	409 days
30×30	30,000 trillion	952,774 years
50×50	25,000 septillion	807 quadrillion years

The shocking conclusion is that the time required to run the program explodes to prohibitive levels as the grid grows. Even a moderate grid size, such as 50×50, would require an enormous amount of time to process—over 50 thousand times the age of the universe.

The relation between the amount of resources needed to run the program and the input size is known as computational *complexity*. In the example above, the resource in question is time, measured against the grid size. In an algorithm with linear complexity, for example, the time required is proportional to the input size: if you double the input, you double the time. The algorithm presented above is much worse than linear: it is factorial, which happens when you go through an exhaustive list of all possible combinations. This is even worse than exponential, which is how epidemics propagate.

Studying the complexity of an algorithm is essential to guarantee that it is possible to satisfy its hunger for resources for any reasonable input size. Complexity deals with how the need for resources grows with the input size and not so much with the specific amount of resources. For example, if you could process ten thousand paths per second instead of one thousand, you would still need five times the age of the universe (as opposed to 50 thousand times) to run the recalculation algorithm. If you could accelerate the algorithm even further, processing 100 thousand paths per second, you would "only" need half the age of the universe, which is still too long to be lost and "recalculating." To beat an algorithm with bad complexity, you need a better algorithm, not a faster computer. That is why algorithm design is a far from trivial task.

The solution described above is very naïve: listing all possibilities and selecting the best one is mere brute force. As early as 1956, Edsger Dijkstra, a Dutch computer scientist, discovered a much more efficient algorithm to find the fastest (or shortest) path through a set of connected nodes. The algorithm first computes fastest paths between nodes that are close to each other and then progressively expands the solution until getting the fastest full path from A to B. Dijkstra's algorithm outputs the same solution as the brute-force approach, with significantly lower complexity. In fact, the time required grows only marginally faster than the input size.

Finding an efficient algorithm is both an art and a science. You may be able to rewrite your problem into a variant of one with a well-known efficient solution and thus benefit from previous research. But sometimes this doesn't work and you just need to get creative. Algorithm design is an important subject in any computer science degree, and you'll find textbooks on the topic spanning thousands of pages.

Sadly, however hard you try, you may not get as lucky as Dijkstra. There are some problems for which it is impossible to find an efficient, non-brute-force solution. This hasn't been exactly proven mathematically, as it is hard to prove a negative, but there are over 3,000 problems for which efficient solutions have not yet been found despite decades of research. There's even an association offering a million dollars to anyone who *proves* that no such solutions exist or, even better, to anyone who finds an efficient solution. For the scope of this book, let's just say that some problems are really hard, or *intractable*, problems for which no efficient algorithms are likely to be found.

An example of an intractable problem is how to calculate the best route to deliver parcels. Let's suppose you own a cargo company and would like to determine the cheapest, shortest or fastest route to deliver parcels to their respective recipients before coming back home at the end of the day. There is no algorithm guaranteed to find the best delivery path in a reasonable time. Your best bet to get an answer to this kind of problem is to use an approximate algorithm, or *heuristic*, which delivers an acceptable result within an acceptable span of time, even if not necessarily the best result. Designing a heuristic is also an art and a science in itself. In the case of the parcel delivery problem, there are well-known approximate algorithms that tend to yield solutions that come as close as 2–3% to the best one. I hope you think of this the next time you get your online shopping delivered in one day.

The running time is just one of the many aspects a programmer needs to consider when designing an algorithm. There are other types of complexity that must be taken into account, such as how memory-hungry, rather than time-hungry, an algorithm is. A modern way to speed up a program is to split it into chunks and run them on different CPU cores simultaneously or even different computers connected through a network. This brings its own challenges to algorithm design: you need to design how to break a problem into pieces and execute them simultaneously, while making sure they don't get in each other's way, and orchestrate the whole process to produce the final answer.

Software development is not just about knowing the programming language. Poor computational complexity is equally poor in all languages. For this reason, it is becoming more and more common in job interviews to let applicants solve a problem in any language they want. The interviewer then asks them to calculate the computational complexity of the solutions proposed and, if they can, come up with more efficient ones.

5

HOW TO SPEAK WITH TECHIES

A while ago, a businessman hired me to develop a prototype of a product that he described something like this: "I want a system that helps companies find opportunities in the news." While this was an idea, it certainly wasn't a computational one. How could I program a computer to find an opportunity without defining what an opportunity was? Think about it: if you had to write a program, line after line, to output "Hey, here's an opportunity!" how would you go about it?

I asked him if he had a specific use case in mind. He got back to me a few days later with a beautifully written case study (not exactly a use case) explaining the target market and its size and why there was a need to improve the current practices with new technology. But it didn't answer the question. I asked him again for a specific example, and his end objectives were as blurry as finding "opportunities" or "value" without defining what they were.

Imagine how different our communication would have been had he said something like, "I want a program that searches for tweets mentioning mergers and acquisitions." That is formulated computationally, meaning you can derive a list of steps to solve the problem.

You can do better than this entrepreneur. Now that you've learned about computing, hardware and software, you should be well equipped to speak with techies. But besides just understanding the computer as a tool, it's best to follow a set of good practices to make communication easier. Over the next few pages, I'll share some tips for effective communication in the world of tech.

COVER THE *HOW*

Before getting too excited about the amazing things you want to achieve with your new product, make sure you've clearly stated the "how." *How* will your business get those amazing results? There is a difference between just expressing your deepest desires ("a travel app with the best user experience") and stating how that will be achieved ("a colored calendar to help identify the cheapest travel dates at a glance"). The latter is much more desirable language as it describes a tech product that can effectively be built.

By stating the how, your directions become actionable: a techie can start to think about what steps it will take to build what you want.

Let's have a look at some examples of non-actionable statements and the way in which focusing on the "how" can make them into actionable goals:

Not actionable	Actionable
Create a search engine that returns really relevant results.	Create a search engine that counts how many other websites have a link to yours to measure your relevance.
Create a website where people can find cheap accommodation.	Create a platform where private individuals can rent a room of their homes to travelers on a budget.
Create an Airbnb for pets.	Create a platform where pet owners who are leaving on vacation can lend their furry friends to avid animal lovers.

This doesn't mean you're doomed to fail if you're not yet able to articulate exactly how your product will work. In fact, speaking to someone with technical expertise may help you shape your business and define the technical idea. For example, after you bring up the need for better relevance in search engine results, a techie could come up with the idea of counting links (which is what Google was built around). But it's always better to go in with a clear set of goals and as clear a path as possible for how to reach them. Your value as a business person is in bringing to the table a market need ("better search engine") and an innovative idea for how to do it.

IDENTIFY THE INPUTS

Whether your clients are entering search words, clicking on buttons, navigating dashboards, or something else, chances are your product will receive input from users. I suggest that you give some thought to exactly how the user will interact with it. You can go as far as sketching the visual interface of your application. If you really know what you want, this should be fairly easy to do. But if it proves hard, you may want to spend some extra time better shaping your idea.

But there are also other inputs to consider. Do you remember when we spoke about the GPS route recalculation algorithm? I mentioned that there was an estimate of how long it would take to drive along each street, based on speed limits, traffic, and other characteristics. But where would you get that data? Can you get it from the city hall? Will you send a surveyor to measure it? Have you collected travel time data from your users' trips in the past?

To build most tech products, you are likely to require external sources of data. And this could be a significant pain point, since data is not always easy to get and you often have to pay for it. The data you get from someone else can also be messy or incomplete.

Your software may also need to connect with the services of other companies in real time. For example, if you're building a travel app, it will have to connect to flight reservation systems to fetch the inventory of available seats and their prices.

To get a clearer picture of the scope of your task, I suggest that, in addition to sketching the user interface, you take some time to list all the different kinds of inputs needed by your application.

IDENTIFY THE OUTPUTS

A few years ago, I spoke with an entrepreneur who wanted my advice on how deep learning methods could be used to do "something" in the transportation sector with CCTV cameras. He had this idea that artificial intelligence could help parse CCTV footage, but he didn't know yet what he wanted to accomplish with it. I told him it was hard for me to help him unless he told me more clearly what he wanted to extract from the footage. He said he would like to build a system to automatically count the number of pedestrians standing on a sidewalk. It was only then, when he defined the output, that we could start a serious discussion about the technical feasibility of the project.

Another way to see this is to think of how you usually describe your business goals. You probably don't create a deck of PowerPoint slides to say that the business should do "something" to become "better" and that sales will "skyrocket." You're more likely to suggest that the advertising budget should increase by X percent in order to gain Y percent market share in the region.

Just try to apply the same principles when defining the outputs of your ideal system. Ask yourself, "What should come out of it and how will I measure if it's good?" In answering this question, try to be as precise and concrete as you can.

CONSIDER YOUR RESOURCES

Always keep in mind that resources are limited. I'm not speaking about money. I mean computational resources: memory and time. In the last chapter, we even saw that a simple program could take millions of years to run if it is designed poorly. For this reason, techies make consequential efforts to design and write an application so that it uses resources efficiently. I suggest that you also keep resource limitations in mind when thinking of your product so that you don't underestimate the effort it will take your techie co-workers to build it.

So, ask yourself, "How memory-hungry is my application?" If you need to process large files, like high-definition video or satellite images, or a huge number of files, like billions of webpages, then it is probably very memory-hungry. This adds a whole new layer of complexity to your application's development. For instance, large files may have to be processed in chunks or a lot of small files may have to be distributed across multiple machines.

Also ask yourself, "How time-sensitive is my application?" This isn't so much about being fast; it is about having a deadline. For example, suppose you own an e-commerce website and would like to show a personalized product recommendation on the homepage, based on a user's previous purchases and the current available inventory. You don't want the user to visit your website and stare at a blank screen for seconds, waiting until the recommendation is generated. That would degrade user experience. So you certainly have a deadline for that task. By how long would you be willing to delay loading the page to include the recommendation? A quarter of a second maybe?

When an application is time-sensitive, coders have to work hard to find clever ways of optimizing the program. And sometimes they even have to make the hard choice of producing suboptimal solutions because they are faster to compute.

For example, suppose that your recommendation system needs to choose from an inventory of millions of products and uses a rather slow AI-based algorithm to identify the best candidate among them. It is likely that the overall process will take too long, and it won't be possible to compute the recommendation in real time (as the users visit the homepage).

In this scenario, techies are likely to suggest what is known as batch processing: precompute the best product for all existing customers every day at midnight and make the results valid for the entire following day. Now every time a user visits the website, the recommended product is just fetched from a file, instead of being computed on the fly, which is much faster. But this comes at a price: the recommendations are only updated once a day and thus do not reflect a customer's most recent orders and the status of the inventory. No complaints to the software developers if a user bought cup noodles and a microwave, and for a few hours the homepage keeps recommending a cookbook.

I hope these tips will help you work with techies more effectively. These recommendations could come in especially handy when you're looking for a technical co-founder for your business. In this search, you need to convince candidates of the potential of your idea, and that's done best when you speak in an actionable language and are aware of some of the potential difficulties of building your product.

PART II

THE INTERNET

6

THE INTERNET

WHAT was the first thing you did this morning, right after you woke up? Did you, like me, pick up your smartphone to scroll through social apps and read the news? Did you put on your smartwatch and ask Siri to check the weather? I bet that within moments of waking up, the Internet was already somehow part of your day. In my case, it took about ten seconds.

Physical objects you'd think would never need the Internet are now "connected." There's even a company selling a connected toaster, in case you made it all the way to breakfast before needing the Internet. And even if you make it beyond breakfast, you can't avoid the Internet much longer once you get to work, where you use email and Google Docs and watch puppy videos on YouTube during your coffee break.

Back in the day, using the Internet was kind of annoying. Do you remember the horrendous noises dial-up made as it connected and how you couldn't make phone calls while online?

I do—but my younger sister is probably oblivious to all of that. She grew up in a time when the Internet had already become pretty much seamless.

Nowadays, when using the Internet, it seems that information flies into your magical smartphone and then back up to the sky. It even seems like content is detached from any physical computer. It's floating up there, "in the cloud."

But, in reality, everything on the Internet lives in a physical machine. When you load a website, your computer connects to another computer somewhere in the world, which sends you the data necessary to render the webpage on your browser. Even when you store your files in the cloud, they reside in a physical computer somewhere in the world, perhaps in a secure underground bunker built by the cloud provider.

There's much more to the Internet than meets the eye. This chapter explains how the Internet works. It will help you understand the complexity behind it and how it is made reliable. It will cover the basics and some common topics I'm sure you've heard of, like domain names and VPNs. The subsequent chapters will discuss aspects of how the Internet is used, including the Web and the cloud, and how content is made secret and kept safe through encryption.

LAYERS

Like everything in the digital world, the Internet was built by stacking several layers of abstraction. At the lowest level sits the physical layer, the devices that transmit signals, including copper wires and Wi-Fi. At the top level sit the applications, such as emails and the Web. Developing the Internet in separate layers enjoys the benefits of division of labor. Electrical engineers, materials scientists and physicists focus on developing mechanisms to transmit data, such as fiber-optic cables or 5G. They do not focus on how that data is used: it may as well encode a top-secret email or images of your favorite Netflix show.

At the other end of the spectrum, software engineers develop the applications that make the Internet useful, such as emails and Web browsers. These use off-the-shelf tools to send data through the Internet without worrying too much about the details of how that is done. These tools are created by engineers at the lower levels of abstraction, who share them upward for others to use.

Over the next few pages, we'll discuss the lower layers responsible for connecting computers. We'll then move up the abstraction ladder, to the mechanisms used to make the Internet reliable.

THE NETWORK OF NETWORKS

How does data physically travel from the machine that hosts a video to your screen when you want to stream it? Or how does it travel from the machine that hosts your business's website to the laptop of a client accessing it?

The data sent throughout the Internet is digital: everything is encoded as a series of ones and zeros. This data is transmitted in three main ways. One of them is through electric pulses over copper wires, which is the case of ADSL, where you connect to the Internet through your phone line. Another way is by means of wireless electromagnetic signals, like light waves but with a wavelength outside the visible spectrum. This includes Wi-Fi and 4G. Finally, fiber-optic cables use intermittent light to send ones and zeros along thin threads of glass or plastic. The light is "trapped" inside the fibers and can thus travel long distances.

It would be impossible to connect all computers in the world to each other directly. The devices in your household, for example, are only directly connected to your home Wi-Fi router. This creates a private home *network* because all your devices can communicate with one another and share resources, like a printer.

When you sign up with an Internet provider, your home network connects to the provider's network and becomes reachable by any other clients of the same provider.

Internet providers that are physically close to each other interconnect their respective networks in common hubs. For example, the London Internet Exchange connects over 800 Internet providers, allowing all their respective customers to communicate with one another. Pairs of providers also often establish one-on-one links to speed things up. The more the providers connect with each other the more this network of networks grows.

To bring this network to a global scale, the resulting regional clusters of Internet providers establish links with other providers overseas. For this, there is a fascinating set of underwater fiber-optic cables connecting all continents. Messages from California can be sent directly to Japan through wires 5,900 miles (9,600 km) long. A message from the U.S. to Australia needs just one stopover in Hawaii. The practice of interconnecting multiple networks is known as inter-networking, which creates a so-called internetwork or internet. The most notable example is, of course, the Internet (with capital I).

THE INTERNET PROTOCOL

The Internet makes it possible for any two members to communicate with each other regardless of their location. But simply having the ability to send messages anywhere isn't enough; there needs to be an agreement, or *protocol*, on how to route and where to deliver the messages. Otherwise, it would be like a mail service with vans and drivers but without addresses, zip codes or schedules. The Internet protocol, or simply IP, defines the set of rules by which data is sent throughout the Internet.

The Internet protocol specifies a way to uniquely identify the different devices throughout the Internet: IP addresses. These consist of four binary numbers of eight digits each. To make them human-readable, they are usually written as four decimal numbers, each between 0 and 255, usually separated by dots. For example, as of today, if I type "172.217.169.46" into my browser, I access Google's website. We will see later on how you can type the much friendlier "google.com" with the same result, but this is only cosmetic: all Internet communication happens through IP addresses.

When your home router connects to the Internet, your provider assigns you a unique IP address from the pool of around 4.3 billion different possible IP addresses. This address usually changes every time you connect, unless you pay to own a dedicated one. Since the assignment of IP addresses is a well-known process and their distribution is overseen by world and regional authorities, you can identify someone's country and Internet provider just by looking at their IP address. Moreover, by accessing the provider's record of which address is attributed to each customer, you could monitor an individual's Internet activity.

Since the devices in the Internet, often known as *nodes*, are not all connected to one another, a message must be routed to the destination through intermediary nodes, which receive and pass on the message to get it closer to its destination. This is just like sending traditional paper mail. When you send a letter to someone in your city, it is first sent to a local distribution center before being redirected to the receiver sometime later. When you send a letter to someone in another city, your local distribution center sends it to a regional distribution center, which is just another warehouse higher up in the hierarchy. From there, it keeps going up to national or international distribution centers, if needed, before going down the ladder all the way to the final destination.

The Internet protocol defines a similar process to route data efficiently through intermediate nodes. The devices that receive packages from a network and forward them to another network are known as *routers*. Think of these as the distribution centers. In order to know what to do with a received message, a router stores a table that indicates which of its neighbors to forward a message to, based on the IP address of the final destination. This is similar to the post office: there is a table in each distribution center that indicates, for each zip code, where to send the letter next, possibly to another distribution center or to the mailman who will deliver it. Routers build and update the routing tables by communicating with their closest neighbors periodically.

The routing tables are designed to forward a package through an efficient route. If you visit a website whose server machine is located in your city, the communication between the two of you will likely never leave the bounds of the city. When you send a file to your Wi-Fi printer, the data never leaves the bounds of your home network. But if you visit a website overseas, an efficient path is chosen to reach the destination through the network of underwater cables, trying to avoid unnecessary travel. Isn't it impressive that all of this happens in the blink of an eye?

The Internet protocol also standardizes the way that data gets packaged to be sent. When you dispatch a regular letter, you put it in an envelope, which has a maximum allowed weight and size, and write the destination and origin addresses on it. In a similar way, the IP protocol requires you to send data in *packets*, which look as follows:

Header	Data
Origin IP, Destination IP, Total length, ...	E.g., 100100100010...

The data part of the packet contains the message you want to send, encoded as a sequence of ones and zeros. The header is an additional piece of data, prepended to the main message, which contains helpful information about the packet, including the origin and destination IP addresses and the total amount of data. If the message exceeds a maximum length, it must be split into multiple packets.

Note that IP is indifferent to what the data in a packet represents or who its sender and receiver are. For example, I'm pretty sure you've heard of servers, which are special machines on the Internet that provide services to clients (the machine that hosts your files in the cloud would be the server, while you are the client). But to the eyes of the Internet, all machines are equal: your laptop and the much more powerful server that stores your iCloud photos are seen as two identical nodes that communicate with each other. In that regard, IP is quite similar to a mail service: all letters are treated equally regardless of the roles of the sender and recipient.

RELIABILITY

The Internet protocol by itself does not incorporate any mechanisms to make sure that a packet makes it to the destination or that the multiple parts of the message arrive in order. It would make a pretty dysfunctional post office on its own: it would require you to split a letter into several smaller ones without sending you acknowledgments of receipt or helping the receiver reconstruct the original message from its parts.

A protocol known as TCP is used to make the Internet reliable. TCP is built around two ideas. First, the data part of an IP packet is used in a smart way to add reliability. The users of TCP agree on how to encode some additional information inside the

content of a message sent through IP. It is like putting another
envelope inside the first envelope:

IP header	IP Data	TCP Header	Data
Origin IP, Destination IP, Total length, ...		Sequence number, Data checksum, ...	100100100010...

The outer envelope looks just like before: an IP header including addresses followed by some data comprising the body
of the message. To the eyes of IP, the data is just a sequence of
numbers to be transported. To the eyes of TCP, the data contains
two parts: a TCP header with additional information to add reliability and the actual message. The TCP header contains a sequence number to help reconstruct the message in order from
the separate packets. This is like opening a letter and finding another envelope inside that says, "Part 1 of 5," or, "Part 2 of 5." The
TCP header also contains a checksum, which is a short number
derived from the message used by the recipient to verify the message wasn't corrupted during transmission. If a checksum newly
computed from the received data doesn't match the one indicated in the header, it means that something went wrong during the
transmission of the data.

The second way of adding reliability in TCP is by defining a
series of steps that sender and receiver should follow to make
sure that the message is delivered properly; this includes sending and expecting acknowledgements of receipt for each packet.
If the sender does not receive an acknowledgment for a packet,
it assumes that it got lost and sends it again. But the acknowl-
edgement of receipt itself could get lost. In that case, the sender would dispatch another copy of the message thinking that it
wasn't delivered successfully. Therefore, the receiver must verify
that there are no duplicates of the same packet, which is easi-

ly done by making sure that no two packets have the same sequence number.

PORT NUMBERS

The TCP protocol introduces an additional functionality to the packets: port numbers. A port is used to identify different applications inside the origin or destination computer. It is akin to indicating that your letter should go to the "Human Resources Department" of a company. The post office only cares about the street address, in order to deliver the letter to the right building. The company has then its own triage system to distribute the correspondence to the relevant divisions. This is the same with IP and TCP, respectively.

Port numbers were added in TCP because IP itself is a bit too naïve: you're never doing just one thing with your computer, so your IP address by itself isn't enough. You're often browsing the Web with multiple tabs open at the same time while reading your emails in Outlook and synchronizing your Dropbox. It wouldn't be very helpful if a message meant to arrive in your Outlook inbox tried to make its way into your Dropbox. The port number in a TCP header is used by the receiver to triage the traffic into the right applications.

In TCP/IP, a full address is indicated by the IP address and the port number, separated by a colon, as in the following example: 127.0.0.1:80. If you haven't dealt with port numbers before, it's because everyone has agreed on the port numbers of the most common applications. For example, a service that returns encrypted webpages is expected to operate on port 443. Typing "https://google.com/" into your browser is the same as typing "https://google.com:443/" because the browser fills in the missing port number for you.

CALCULATED UNRELIABILITY

The reliability provided by TCP is overkill in certain applications. For example, video calls require data to be delivered as fast as possible, even at the expense of losing some of it. There is an alternative protocol for this, known as UDP, which is less reliable than TCP but faster. It provides port numbers and some basic checksums, but it does not require acknowledgments of receipt and a lot of the overhead that comes with TCP. It is thus popular in streaming applications, where it's important to give a sense of real-time communication.

BEAUTIFYING IP ADDRESSES

Imagine having to type "172.217.169.46" into your browser every time you wanted to Google something. Most of us couldn't remember that number, and even if we did, we would also have to remember where "172.217.169.46" takes us. We are all much more familiar with human-friendly domain names, such as google.com.

But every time you refer to a domain name, your computer needs to find the matching IP address because that is the only type of address supported by the Internet protocol. This mapping from domain names to IP addresses is done by referencing the domain name system (DNS), akin to calling the operator to find someone's phone number. There are dedicated machines all around the world, known as DNS servers, whose purpose is to perform that translation.

When you connect to the Internet, your provider sends you the IP address of a preferred DNS server, for example, 208.67.222.222. When you type "mystore.co.uk" into your browser for the first time, there is no record of its corresponding IP address. In order to find it, your computer sends a request to 208.67.222.222, querying "mystore.co.uk."

The DNS server now has the task of *resolving* the IP address for you. It would be very hard for a single server to store and maintain an up-to-date table for the millions of domain names that exist. The server thus communicates with other DNS servers in the world, which are organized hierarchically, until hitting the right record.

At the top of the hierarchy there are 13 root servers operated by 12 different organizations and supported by 1,000 machines worldwide. Since the IP addresses to reach them are well known to everyone, they constitute a good point to start the search.

The root servers do not reply with the final result but refer you to the IP address of another server in charge of handling the rightmost part of the domain of interest, such as ".uk" or ".com." In the case of "mystore.co.uk," you will now know who to query about ".uk" domains, to which you send a new request. After a couple more steps, you will hopefully obtain the IP address you were looking for, and only then you can start the TCP/IP communication with the website.

To make the process less cumbersome, your browser will remember the retrieved IP address and doesn't require a new DNS look-up on every subsequent visit to that website. The memorized IP addresses expire, typically after 24 hours, in order to adapt to potential changes. That is why if you migrate your website to a different IP address, it may take a while for your users to hit the right location. Web browsers implement other creative solutions to minimize the time spent waiting for DNS look-ups. For example, while you are reading a webpage that contains links to other domains, your browser performs their DNS look-ups in the meantime, in case you click on any of them.

THE SCARCITY OF IP ADDRESSES

There are about four billion possible IP addresses, which doesn't sound future-proof considering a global population of nearly eight billion people and an ever-increasing number of connected devices per person. That is why your Internet provider gives you only one IP address for your entire household, which is shared among all the devices. When you connect to the Wi-Fi of a coffee house, you share a single IP address with everyone else in the venue. This is the *external* IP address, used to identify the coffee house, and not the individual devices, in the outside world.

The devices behind an external IP address also get a unique address. But these are private and only used to identify the devices inside the home or coffee house and let them communicate with each other. For example, when you send a file from your laptop to your Wi-Fi printer, its private IP address is used. These are unique inside your network but may be repeated in different networks. Two people in different coffee houses may have the same private IP address, but since the networks are independent, this is not a problem. If you send a file to a printer whose address in your network is "192.168.1.10," it will reach the right printer even if other people's printers are also "192.168.1.10" in their respective networks. No external communication via the Internet takes place in this scenario.

Things are a bit more complicated when a device inside your network needs to communicate with the outside world. In this case, the router funnels all the incoming requests from different devices into the single external IP address. It does so by overriding the internal IP addresses with the external one. It also overrides the origin port number to avoid collisions from two applications in different devices that use the same port, for instance if you were browsing the Web from both your smartphone and your laptop. The following figure shows an example of this process:

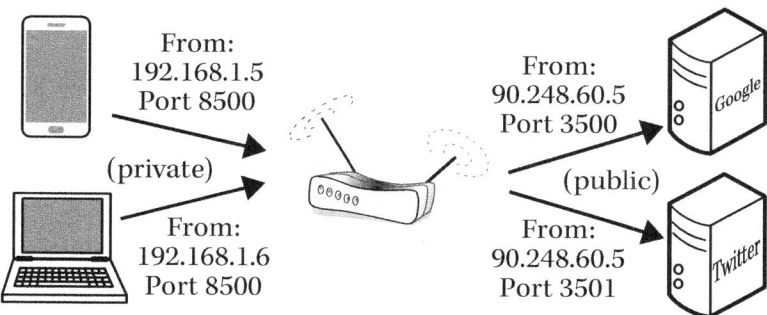

When getting a response, the router redirects it to the right machine:

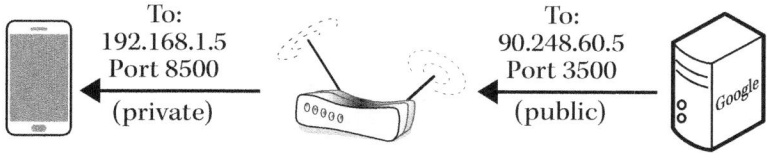

For this, the router maintains a translation table with the correspondences between internal IP addresses and port numbers into the external ones. This method, known as network address translation (NAT), is routinely used to give Internet access to large private networks, such as an entire office, through a single external IP address. This increases the potential of the otherwise scarce four billion addresses.

As early as 1998, the designers of the Internet protocol realized that the four billion limit would soon become a problem. As a response, they developed a new version of the IP protocol, known as IP version 6, or IPv6, which has longer addresses. The new protocol allows a total of approximately 340 trillion trillion trillion different addresses, a number that contains 37 zeros. This should more than solve the scarcity problem.

In 2012, there was a highly publicized event, known as World IPv6 Day, in which several Web giants activated IPv6 on their main websites to encourage adoption of the protocol. As of 2020, while some steady progress has been made, the majority of Internet traffic is still carried out over the old version of IP, with its short and scarce addresses.

VIRTUALLY PRIVATE

When you send an IP packet, any intermediate nodes, or even someone tapping into the wires, can know who the packet is coming from and who it's intended for. In encrypted communication, the message is made illegible to unintended readers by scrambling its content, which we will discuss later on in this book. But this is only done on the content of the message and not the header containing the origin and destination addresses. If you made the addresses illegible, no one would know where it is supposed to go and it wouldn't be successfully routed to its final destination. In a similar way, if you want to send a secret message to a friend through traditional mail, you may use an agreed cryptic code to write the letter, but you still need to write your friend's address in a legible way on the envelope.

Since the origin IP address of a packet is visible, Netflix can infer the country in which you are located and only let you watch the shows available there. Since the destination address is also visible, an oppressive government can block any requests you send to a censored website.

There is a way to overcome these restrictions. Suppose you want to pretend you are located in France. You can send your IP packets to your French friend Vincent Pierre Nolibois (VPN) and ask him to resend those packets to a desired destination as if they were his. Inside the original packets you leave a note for Vincent indicating where the messages should be sent to.

The packets resent by Vincent are genuinely issued from France and have no signs of their real origin. Vincent then forwards you any responses he receives that are intended to you. This is how you can hide your identity and country of origin. You can also hide the actual content that you're fetching from the Internet. For example, if you wanted to visit Facebook in a country where Facebook is censored, you can pretend that you're just communicating with your French friend Vincent, who will forward your messages to Facebook and send you back any responses as if they came from him.

There are countless commercial providers of this kind of message forwarding service, known as VPNs, which is not a Frenchman's initials but stands for virtual private networks. It is still possible, though not easy, to guess your identity when you are using a VPN. For example, if someone could snoop into all the communication Vincent has with his friends, they could see that you're communicating a lot with him and blow your cover. But this is hard to do and would involve espionage in foreign territory. In any case, you could add more intermediary friends along the way to make the process more robust. The drawback is that, when using a VPN, the messages have to travel longer distances around the world and their delivery becomes slower.

If Vincent's service becomes popular, it won't take long until everyone knows that he is a VPN and his traffic is not actually his. The IP addresses of known VPNs are thus routinely blacklisted by those who apply restrictions. Bypassing Internet blockages requires you to go through an intermediary but one that isn't known to be one.

VPNs weren't invented to let you watch your favorite Netflix show while you're abroad. They can be much more powerful than that. Remember that the devices in your household or your office form a private network, allowing you to share resources like a printer. These devices can also benefit from a shared layer of security, such as a firewall that blocks suspicious websites. But when you're working from home, you're connected to your home network and can't access the resources of the office. You are able to print with your home printer but not send a file to the printer inside the office building for a colleague to pick up. You are also more vulnerable to cyberattacks because the security measures implemented at your home network are probably not as thorough as the corporate ones.

Companies routinely use VPNs to extend their private networks to remote locations without having a direct physical link. This is why, when you work from home, your company might ask you to "connect to the VPN." From then on, any outgoing packet is first encapsulated and sent to your company's private network. Then the packet is handled as if you were physically connected to that network. This way, you can enjoy all the benefits of corporate security and shared printing while working from home.

7

THE WEB

THERE are countless ways in which the Internet can be used to communicate data. But one of them stands out above all: the Web.

The Web is an information system, built on top of the Internet, used to share content such as text and images, which are known as Web resources. It also introduces an innovative type of resource, the webpage. Webpages are unlike any other document—they can be animated and contain links to other pages. To create them, the Web has its own set of languages (perhaps you've heard of HTML?).

The Web has become a ubiquitous part of our lives. In fact, when was the last time you *installed* software in your laptop? That's how it used to be: you'd get a dedicated piece of software for each thing you wanted to do. You would buy an entire encyclopedia that came in many CDs and install it in your machine.

But things have changed since then. Now you spend a lot of your computer time in front of a Web browser, such as Safari or Chrome, rather than using purpose-specific applications. Even when you want to multiply two numbers, you just type it into

Google. Instead of using dedicated computer applications, we now run sophisticated software through Web browsers. These pieces of software are known as Web applications, or Web apps.

This chapter will answer many of your questions about how the Web and Web apps work and how they are built. Have you ever seen the title *front-end developer* in a job ad, for example, and wondered what that was about? Or have you ever wondered how, as you scroll down your social media feed, new posts keep appearing at the bottom of the page endlessly? You'll soon find out.

WEB SERVERS

When you navigate the Web, you constantly ask for Web resources from the machines that host them, known as Web servers.

You can set up a Web server in your own laptop and host your website there, but it is impractical. For example, if your computer turned off for some reason, the website would stop working. In general, you would hire dedicated infrastructure from a Web hosting provider.

When you interact with a Web server, you communicate using a protocol known as HTTP. This protocol defines a common way to identify resources with addresses, or URLs, and how to send messages to request those resources. For example, suppose you type "http://www.example.com/faq.html" into your browser. First, your browser establishes a connection with the server that hosts example.com by using its IP address and the mechanisms seen in the last chapter. Then the browser sends an HTTP request that looks like this:

GET /faq.html **HOST** www.example.com

In plain English, this says, "I want you to get me a resource called '/faq.html' from a website called 'www.example.com', which is hosted in your machine." The server replies with the relevant content.

In the early days of the Web, a website was a collection of static webpages, such as "About us" and "Frequently asked questions." These were stored as individual files inside the hard drive of a server, which would send them to you upon request. Nowadays, as we'll see in a minute, a server often constructs the Web content on the fly and tailors it to you.

THE FRONT END

The *front end* of a Web application is the part that is processed inside the end user's computer, instead of the Web server. For example, when you access a webpage, the server doesn't send you the content as you see it on your screen. It sends you a plain text file instead with hints on how to style its content into a prettier format. It is then the task of your browser to interpret that content and render it on the screen, giving it its intended look and feel. Since the job is done inside your computer, rendering webpages is part of the front end.

The text files used to represent and stylize webpages are written in a special language known as HTML. Any web-based business is likely to have a lot of HTML in its products, so let me show you how it works. Let's start with a simple example of HTML:

<h1> My beautiful header </h1>
My text.

This is vanilla text. If you open it on any text editor, such as Notepad, you'll see the bland text from above. But this file has been enriched by adding *tags* to indicate the function and style of elements in your document. In this case, the text "My beautiful header" has been enclosed between two tags: "<h1>" and "</h1>," which indicate, respectively, the beginning and end of a header. The *h* is for header, and the *1* indicates that it's the most important level of header: a title.

Let's say you write this in a text editor and save it as a file called "webpage.html." Now, instead of using a text editor, you open the file with your Web browser. You can try this at home. The Web browser will show you this:

My beautiful header

My text

The browser made the tags disappear and used them to style the first line of the document. Since it understood that the first line is a title, it increased the size of the text, which is the default behavior for titles unless stated otherwise.

If you'd prefer a red title instead, you can modify the first line of the file as follows:

<h1 style="color:red"> My beautiful red header </h1>

The resulting webpage looks exactly like the one above but has a red title instead. This simple procedure is how webpages are written. There exist many more tags, other than the basic "h1" and "color:red," allowing you to create highly stylized webpages. For example, sophisticated tags are used to automatically adapt the layout to different screen sizes.

Every request for a webpage is answered with HTML text, used by the browser to beautify and format the content on the screen. But if HTML is just plain text with tags, how can webpages have images in them?

In order to add an image, you need to include a snippet of

HTML text that points to the URL of an image, as in the following example:

```
<img src="myimage.jpg">
```

When your browser stumbles upon this tag, it sends another HTTP request to the server asking for the resource "myimage.jpg." The server replies with the image file and the browser renders it at the right location on the page. That explains why, sometimes, the text of a webpage loads first and the images come next.

Links to other websites are also created through enriched plain text:

```
<a href="http://another_example.com/"> Click here </a>
```

For that line of text, the browser only shows "Click here" on the screen. But if you click on the link, the browser takes you to the linked website by sending a new HTTP request for its content (to "http://another_example.com/").

Imagine your website contains several pages ("About us," "Contact us," "Meet the team," etc.) and you want to apply a unified style, such as a red header on each of them. You could add *style="color:red"* every time a header appears on every page. But if someone decided to change all the headers to blue, you'd have to modify them one by one. This is not a sustainable way of writing a website. A better solution is to create a single file that describes style and invoke that style in every HTML page to adopt it. The style file, called a *cascading stylesheet*, or CSS, looks like this:

```
h1 {color: red;}
```

This indicates in quite a readable way that a header's color should be red. A special tag is then used in each HTML page to tell the browser where to fetch this stylesheet. When the browser finds that tag, it sends an extra request to the server to get the stylesheet and beautifies the webpage accordingly. Has it ever happened to you that you opened a webpage and it looked really ugly, with only black text on a white background? This is especially true when you have poor Wi-Fi coverage. A few seconds later, or after you hit "refresh," the page becomes much more stylish. This is because, the first time, the HTML was loaded fine but there was a problem with fetching the separate stylesheet.

MAKING THE FRONT END INTERACTIVE

A contemporary webpage is not just static content for you to read, as in a paper magazine. It is often interactive or animated. For example, the color of a button changes just by hovering over it with your mouse pointer. Or you expand a list by clicking on "+" and hide it by clicking on "–." There are also messages that pop up when you load a page, saying, "Please, subscribe," which you can ignore by clicking on "x" or "No, I don't want free advice." These actions happen inside a single webpage without loading a new one.

To add interactivity, browsers can be configured to modify pieces of the HTML page based on user actions. Programmers do this by embedding snippets of code in a programming language known as JavaScript (which doesn't have anything to do with the Java programming language, by the way).

For example, suppose you want to change the color of the title to red when the user clicks a button; let's have a look at the code needed to achieve that.

First, you write an HTML webpage with a title and a button that says, "Click me":

```
<h1> My beautiful header </h1>
<button> Click me </button>
```

If you write this in your text editor and open it with your browser, you'll see the following:

My beautiful header

Click me

Since the button is not connected to any action, clicking on it has no effect. You need to modify the second line of the HTML file to indicate that an action should be taken:

```
<button onclick="change_color()"> Click me </button>
```

You don't need to understand the details of this line, but in plain English it says, "When someone clicks on this button, execute the JavaScript function called change_color, specified later on."

At the end of the HTML file you add your JavaScript functionality, enclosed between "script" tags:

```
<script>
   function change_color() {
      document.getElementsByTagName("h1")[0].
      style.color = "red";}
</script>
```

Once again, you don't have to fully understand this code, but in plain English it says, "From the HTML document, get the first h1 header, access its style, and change its color to red." And *voilà*. You can try this at home: if you put these pieces of code in your notepad, save it as a .html file and open it with your browser, you will see that clicking on the button effectively changes the color of the title, from the default black to red.

An actual website typically contains more sophisticated dynamism than that. You can zoom into a stock price chart or filter the flights in your search results for "non-stop only." All of these actions are implemented by inserting JavaScript code that manipulates the HTML document.

JavaScript is a fully functional language. It can be used to do anything, including complex calculations. But the JavaScript code embedded in a webpage is executed by the browser in the machine of the end-user (it is part of the front end, remember?). Therefore, you can't ask too much of a piece of JavaScript code or it could become too slow to run in the client's personal computer. You may also want to avoid running anything that is potentially unsafe in the user's machine. That's why JavaScript is typically reserved for cosmetic tasks and not for heavy duty jobs.

THE BACK END

Not all the content on the Web is static, like a "Terms and Conditions" page, written once and dumped as a file in the Web server. For example, when you visit "My orders" on an online store, you see a history of all the things you, and not someone else, have ordered from the store. This, of course, doesn't mean that there is someone writing a different HTML page for each user and updating it every time an order is placed.

This is an example of a dynamic website, in which, once your request is received, a program inside the server *assembles* the output for you in real time. A lot of things happen during this assembly, including accessing a database with your most recent shopping orders. To the eyes of your browser, the assembled webpage it receives looks the same as static HTML. Nothing indicates that the page was assembled for you by a program rather than written by hand, line by line.

The server-side software that dynamically assembles content behind the scenes is known as the *back end*. The overall architecture of an imaginary shopping Web app would look as follows:

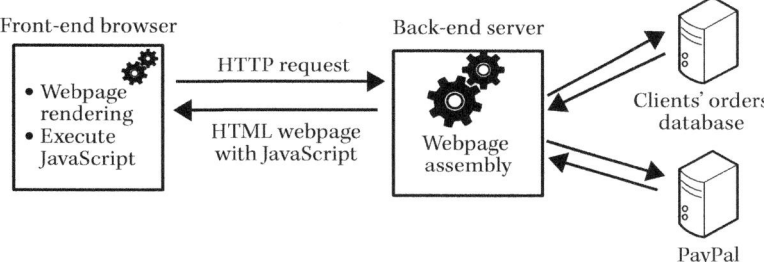

The front end is in charge of rendering the webpage and modifying it by executing JavaScript. All of this happens in the client's computer. The back end, which runs in the server, is in charge of running a program to assemble the webpage. A lot of things may happen during this assembly, such as accessing a database containing the clients' shopping orders. The back end may also communicate with external services, like PayPal to process payments.

The heavy-duty work typically happens in the back end. For example, when you ask Google Maps through your browser to find directions from A to B, the calculation of the best route is performed inside Google's powerful back-end servers. The route is then sent back to your browser, which simply displays it.

In the old days, the dedicated GPS device in your car was itself in charge of computing the best route. Since these devices were not even connected to the Internet, you had to store in them the relevant maps and update them periodically. The calculation of routes was quite slow and, of course, unaware of live traffic conditions. Now the process has become significantly quicker and up to date, not necessarily because smartphones are faster but because the task has been outsourced to the back end.

In a similar way, when you ask something to Siri, the voice recording is sent to an Apple server, where the speech is processed and analyzed and the answer sent back to you. A lot of the processing that once happened in the end user's device has now been moved to back-end servers, where processing can happen more quickly.

THE WORLD OF WEB APIS

As we've seen, Web servers respond to HTTP requests, like when someone types your website's address into the browser. But you can also allow the Web apps of other businesses to make requests to your server and thus offer them your complex back-end functionality.

To avoid any confusion in this process, the back-end engineers publish a specification of all they have to offer and how to send the requests, like a shopping catalog. This specification is known as an API. By knowing each other's APIs, the Web apps of different businesses can communicate with one another and use one another's back-end functionality.

For example, Twitter offers a public API to retrieve historical tweets mentioning a certain subject. By following the instructions of this API, another business can send HTTP requests and retrieve tweets to use in their own Web apps. This way, you could create your own social media analytics company that connects to Twitter to retrieve data. Similarly, travel agencies use APIs from airlines and car rental agencies to fetch their inventory and make reservations on behalf of their customers.

Instead of replying with stylized HTML, the functionality provided through Web APIs typically returns a raw representation of the content needed. This is because the task of presenting and beautifying the text is left to the consumers of the content, who stylize it to the look of their own websites. For example, the description of a flight returned by an API looks something like this:

{"flight number": "1234", "price": "130 dollars", "airline": "United"}

This contains information about the flight, including the price and airline, but no HTML style tags.

Web APIs are also commonly used to outsource tasks in real time to external service providers, for a fee. And, believe me, there is an API for everything. For example, there are several companies who provide services to detect nudity and inappropriate content in images. You send them the image via a request to the server, and they assess the appropriateness of the picture by using their proprietary image recognition algorithms. The response is sent back to you almost immediately. This external service could be used, for example, to assess the appropriateness of the content users post in your forum. This spares you the need for writing yourself a method to detect nudity, while you also benefit from the outstanding proprietary technology created by someone who specializes in that awkward task.

There are also APIs for simple tasks like validating email addresses. For example, you can use a service provided through an external API to make sure that your users enter correct email addresses on the contact form (e.g., must contain "@" and finish in ".com"). All you need is to send an HTTP request in the correct form with the email address in question, and the server replies with its assessed validity status.

Public APIs are usually billed by the number of requests, with prices going as low as a few cents per million requests. They usually require you to send an agreed secret key as part of the request, to prove you're authorized to use the API, and limit the number of requests you can send within a period of time. Next time you need to add functionality to your Web app, you may want to check beforehand if someone else provides an API to do what you need. You'll have to assess whether you're okay with paying for it or you'd rather develop it in-house.

As you can see, in the world of Web APIs, the act of accessing a webpage may look like a single request, but it often triggers a cascade of other requests that travel around the globe.

THE SCIENCE BEHIND GIVING LIKES

If you remember the old days of the Web, a lot of time was spent loading and reloading webpages. Every action that required interaction with the server resulted in loading a new page. For example, online maps were static images. They came with four arrow buttons (North, South, East and West) and two buttons with magnifying glasses ("+" and "-") used to navigate the map. Every time you clicked on one of those buttons, an entirely new page was loaded with the new image tile, showing a different area of the map. Pressing any of these buttons had a similar effect to navigating a news website: on every click you were sent to a different webpage that was loaded from scratch.

This is no longer the case. When you navigate through Google Maps, you can zoom in and scroll through different areas of the earth without leaving and returning to the page again and again. But the user can't have a copy of the map of the entire earth, so there must be an extra hidden communication between the page and the back end to fetch relevant map tiles on the fly.

In a similar fashion, when you give a "like" to a Facebook post, you do not need to wait until the entire Facebook page is reloaded for that like to register. The color of the button changes with immediate effect to signal the like, and you never leave the page.

We've seen that changing colors is easy with JavaScript. However, there must be some hidden communication with Facebook's server because it needs to be notified about the like; otherwise, the writer of the post would never know you liked it or the like wouldn't be there anymore when you came back later.

In addition to modifying the visuals of a webpage, JavaScript code is also capable of sending hidden HTTP requests to the back end. When you give a like on Facebook, the JavaScript code attached to the "click" event, in addition to changing the style of the button, sends a hidden HTTP message to the server to notify that you've liked the post. The response from the server is then intercepted by JavaScript and used to alter the content of the page accordingly. Since this happens behind the scenes, it doesn't require you to reload the webpage. This pattern is known as AJAX and was first popularized by the online travel agency Kayak.com and Google, with Gmail and Google Maps. The following is a toy example of a Facebook-like Web app with an additional hidden AJAX connection between a webpage's JavaScript and the back end:

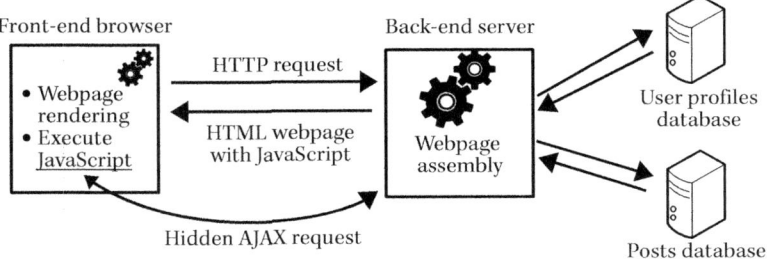

This pattern is also used to retrieve data from the server, such as more map tiles or more Facebook posts. When you're scrolling down through your Facebook feed, there's a point at which you reach the last post of the page. When this happens, JavaScript code sends a hidden request to Facebook's servers, asking for a new batch of posts, which are then appended to the bottom of the feed. Sometimes this takes a few seconds, during which you're shown the silhouette of an empty post to indicate that you're waiting for more content to come. You don't need to load a new page to see more posts, making it look like an infinite page. This is the same mechanism used by Google Maps to fetch more tiles as you navigate the map.

THE PROFESSIONS OF THE WEB

Back-end and front-end Web development require different skills and are thus usually taken care of by separate professionals.

Front-end developers use HTML, CSS stylesheets and JavaScript to write the software that is executed on the end user's computer. There's no wiggle room to choose languages, since these are the ones that all browsers understand. Front-end developers are concerned with the presentation and interactivity of the Web app. They use dedicated libraries and frameworks to make their lives easier. For example, React is a very popular open-source framework developed by Facebook that makes it easy for the different components of a webpage to interact with each other. Front-end developers are programmers but not necessarily designers: they take the visual concept envisioned by a Web designer and implement it into a functional app.

You are probably used to designing visuals by dragging and dropping things, as when creating a PowerPoint presentation. It may seem strange that a front-end developer writes code in order to define the style of a website. Wouldn't it be easier to use a drag-and-drop tool?

Those tools do exist. They are known as WYSIWYG ("what you see is what you get"). They let you drag and drop items, increase text size, change the colors and so on, all with a couple of clicks, and they automatically generate the underlying HTML code for the webpage. However, they are hardly ever used by professional developers, who prefer to "code" the design. This is because, in the long run, a developer prefers to have absolute control over the HTML code, instead of accepting the decisions of the visual editor. After gaining some experience, it also becomes easier to get the exact desired effect by writing the specific code than by dragging and dropping boxes. Moreover, the design of a website is not just about its looks. JavaScript is used to add interactivity, and HTML tags must be used cleverly to identify the meaning of each component of the website, which can get more complicated than just headers and text. Well-chosen HTML tags make your website friendly to the search engines that scan it and make it easy to factor out common style elements in a separate stylesheet.

On the flip side, back-end developers write the software that runs behind the scenes, in the innards of a Web server. They are responsible for writing the program that dynamically assembles the webpage that is sent to the user. They are also responsible for designing and writing the Web API that responds to requests from the front end or other back-end servers.

The languages used for the back end are usually the same as in conventional programming of desktop applications, such as Java and Python. One of the main differences between coding for the Web and for a desktop application is the interface: the back end of the Web responds to HTTP requests, while a desktop program responds to user clicks and keyboard strokes. Back-end developers use dedicated libraries and frameworks to assist their work, including tools to authenticate users or send emails automatically. They also connect with databases and external services, like an airline's reservation system.

The rare professionals with expertise in both sides of Web apps are known as full-stack developers.

THE IMPORTANCE OF WEB ARCHITECTURE

As we've seen, the software of a Web app runs in two different places: the server and the end client's browser. In general, the heavy-duty processing is done in the back end, and the presentation is taken care of in the front end. But the line is not always clear cut. Sometimes the back end handles a part of the presentation, and the front end performs complex calculations before displaying the result. So where should the line be drawn between front end and back end?

There is no right answer to this question: there are different ways to split the tasks between front end and back end. The process of making this kind of decision is known as *Web architecture*. There are different models, each with its own pros and cons. Whatever the decision, it must be made with a lot of care. Once a Web app's architecture has been designed, the app has been developed, and it is live serving thousands of users per minute, it is hard to go back on the initial decisions.

8

NAVIGATING THE WEB

Now that you we've seen how the Web works, let's have a look at some common topics that are likely to arise when you're doing business in the field. I'm talking about Web scraping, search engines, cookies and mobile apps.

WEB SCRAPING

A user navigates the Web by constantly sending requests and receiving responses. This process can be automated in a program, or "robot," to simulate the interactions of a human and collect data. You could do this to automatically track the prices of your competitors, for example.

This practice, known as Web scraping, can go as far as simulating the entire journey of a customer. For example, the robot visits the website of a competing travel agency, enters the destination and dates of travel, selects an airline and a hotel, and retrieves the price of a package holiday. It records that data and then repeats the same process thousands of times over to gather all of your competitors' prices.

To write a robot, you need to understand how the front end of the website works. This is easy to do, since the code is sent to your machine and executed there. If you right-click on a web-page and select "inspect," your browser opens a panel that shows the underlying HTML and JavaScript code, exactly as written by the Web developers. This is, of course, only true for the code that runs in your machine and not for the back-end code, which is kept secret in the servers.

Knowing the front end makes it easy to understand how the user interface works and to simulate the browsing process with a robot. You just need to write a program that automatically sends HTTP requests as a human would do. The only impediment would be if there is a CAPTCHA that asks you to solve a problem to prove that you're not a robot, like entering the characters of a distorted image. Since this is rarely enforced, most of the Web is scrapable. This isn't effortless though. For example, every time a website changes its structure or the way it's navigated, you have to modify the robot accordingly.

But the fact that you can browse the Web automatically doesn't mean you're allowed to do it. Southwest Airlines used to offer a refund if a client detected that the price of a flight dropped after purchasing it. In 2017, a website called SWMonkey offered a service that tracked the price of a flight purchased. If the price dropped, it would send a notification to the passenger and take a commission on the refund. But the "Terms and Conditions" section of Southwest Airline's website, as is the case with most websites, explicitly forbids unauthorized scraping by robots. It didn't take long for SWMonkey to disappear, a couple of lawsuits later.

If your business idea revolves around automatically collecting data from the Internet, I advise you to consider the legality of doing so. You could get going for a while, when the business is small and no one notices; but the moment you try to scale up the business, the scraped websites may want to charge you for their data or outright prohibit you from collecting it. This could invalidate your entire business model. In general, when a business wants to openly share data with robots, they provide a friendly Web API to do so, eliminating the need for scraping content in the first place.

Businesses built around offering content from someone else are, in general, explicitly authorized to do so. For example, a flight meta-search engine such as Skyscanner has individual agreements with travel agencies to access their prices. In fact, the agencies pay a commission to Skyscanner for its referrals. The moral of the story is that while you may be able to scrape the Web for useful data, it is best only to do so through authorized means like APIs.

SEARCH ENGINES

The ultimate Web scraper is Google, or search engines in general, which periodically visit millions of websites to index their content. You can think of a search engine as comprising two separate lists. The first list contains the addresses of known webpages (they cannot "search the Web" without knowing where to look).

When you create a new website, no search engine knows about its existence automatically. Search engines constantly navigate, or *crawl*, the Web to expand their list of existing webpages. Whenever they find a link to a new unknown page, they add it to the list of known resources. Therefore, the best way of appearing in a search engine is to have others link to your content. Some search engines also provide a way of notifying them when new content is created.

The second list built by a search engine is an index of search terms. For example, it contains an entry with the word "airplane" and a list of webpages that mention that word. This index is constructed by scraping the content of the known webpages. When you update a webpage, it takes a while until the crawler pays it a visit and indexes the new content.

When you run a search, the engine references this index to bring up relevant search results. This is as opposed to visiting the webpages themselves when you perform a search, which would be really slow. Search algorithms have, of course, become increasingly sophisticated, tolerating misspellings or expanding the results by including related terms from the index.

Most websites, in their terms and conditions, allow scraping if it is done by search engines. Who wouldn't like to be found on Google, after all? But it is possible to avoid that by adding a file called "robots.txt" to your website's server. This file, which should be written in an agreed format, lists the things robots are authorized to do with the content and can be used to tell search engines to back off.

Probably the most intriguing aspect of a search engine is its search and relevance algorithm, which decides which results to show for a query and in which order. Google was built around the idea of analyzing the external links that point to a website to assess its authority. The more other sites link to a website, the more authoritative that website is deemed to be. At the same time, the more mentions of the search term in a page, the more it is considered to be a relevant result.

Getting unpaid, or *organic*, traffic from Google search results is the Holy Grail of online marketing. The practice of improving a website to position it at the top of the search results is known as *search engine optimization*, or SEO. The SEO specialist will be familiar with Google's latest guidelines for an optimal placement in their search results. For example, it is important to have a mobile version of the website that works well on small screens. Having text embedded in images isn't a good idea since Google can't easily read the content, and so on.

In the past, the older versions of the Google algorithm were easily manipulated. There was a whole branch of SEO, infamously known as "black-hat" SEO, which used questionable practices to position a website on Google. It spammed the Web with bogus links and crowded a webpage with target keywords to trick Google's algorithm and improve the relevance of a website. Sometimes the SEO specialist would put a long list of white keywords on a white background at the end of a page, which was invisible to the end user but fooled Google's algorithm.

Google introduced a series of reforms that drastically eliminated these conniving practices and penalized the websites that implemented them, bringing them to the bottom of the search results. The reforms were so brutal that their code names are well-known to the community: Panda, Penguin, Hummingbird, and the names of other adorable animals. A lot of websites that made money through advertisement but provided little value to the readers saw their revenue wiped out by the reforms.

Now Google's algorithm has become highly sophisticated. It is fair to say that it can tell when content is genuinely useful to the user. It's still a good idea to optimize a website, making it search engine-friendly, but the days of messing with Google's algorithm are long gone.

COOKIES

Without cookies, your browsing experience would be very different. A cookie is a piece of data sent by the server along with a website's data and stored in a user's computer.

Cookies are the reason you stay logged in to a website instead of having to type your password again and again with every visit. Right after a successful login, the server sends you a cookie containing a secret key, which is stored in your machine. From then on, your browser includes that secret key as part of any request to the same server. Since you're the only one in possession of that key, the server knows that the request is really coming from you and doesn't ask for your password again.

Cookies are also used to remember your selection of language and currency, even when you come back days later. They are also used to hold the products in your shopping cart until you check out. That's why you can keep browsing a store and adding more products to your cart without emptying it every time you visit a new page. These kinds of cookies are an essential part of the browsing experience and are unlikely to disappear anytime soon.

But cookies came under public scrutiny due to a different, somewhat controversial kind of use. By default, browsers only let a cookie be read by the same domain that generated it. For example, a cookie stored by facebook.com can only be accessed by facebook.com. Otherwise, the consequences would be catastrophic. Imagine if a website could easily read the authentication cookie from another website: they could steal it and log in to your account.

But there's a trick: it is quite common for webpages to embed third-party content, and that third party can now store cookies under its name. For example, when you embed a YouTube video in a webpage, YouTube can store cookies that belong to them and will thus be readable by them later on. These are known as third-party cookies.

Suppose you visit ten different websites and each of them contains an advertisement generated by an ad platform, like Google Ads. Each of the visits leaves a trail in the form of a third-party cookie, accessible by the ad platform. Later on, when you visit an eleventh website with an ad in it, the ad platform uses your browsing history, found in the cookies, to generate an ad especially targeted to you. This is one of the ways in which ads follow you around the Web—you look at a product page on an online store and then see ads for the same product when visiting other, unrelated websites.

Third-party cookies have created significant controversy because some people are not comfortable with websites collecting their browsing history, especially without their consent. In response, most Web browsers have now either disabled third-party cookies by default or are planning to do so in the near future. The European Union addressed the issue by introducing a regulation that requires websites to get consent from users before storing sensitive cookies. Since then, a window pops up when you visit most websites, asking you to approve or not the use of cookies.

But this doesn't mean the end of targeted advertisement. In particular, Google Chrome is developing new ways to still make targeting possible while also protecting privacy. For example, one of their suggestions is for the browser itself to assign the user to an interest category, such as "traveler," and make this general information available to advertisers but not to provide a user's detailed browsing history. This is an on-going development, and we will only know in a few years where things go.

MOBILE APPS

On desktop and laptop computers, it has become rare to install dedicated software applications: more and more is done through the Web browser. But the world of mobile devices is a different story. You constantly install *apps* on your smartphone, for everything from Facebook to Uber. With few exceptions, like the calculator, most mobile apps interact with the Web.

The reason for writing dedicated mobile apps is to integrate the device's capabilities gracefully, such as push notifications, the GPS and Face ID. Programming an app is done pretty much like traditional software, using languages like Java (as opposed to the Web toolset, such as HTML). The apps interact with the Web by sending requests to the back-end servers, just like webpages do.

But mobile app developers suffer from the same problems

as those writing desktop software: you need to create several versions of the same app, adapted to each of the possible platforms, such as Android and iOS. That explains why apps are often available for Android but not for iOS, and vice versa.

An app that is programmed specifically for Android or iOS is known as *native*. The alternative is to take one step up in the degree of abstraction and use a cross-platform framework, which provides a set of tools to code an app once and adapt it to the different platforms.

The earliest cross-platform technologies often yielded slow and unsatisfactory results. They worked solely with the common features of all environments, which meant you couldn't fully exploit the individual features of each of them. An iPhone app ended up not looking like a "real" iPhone app. Facebook's CEO said that the biggest mistake they'd made as a company was to bet on cross-platform technology over native. The early cross-platform Facebook app was slow and clunky, which led them to develop native apps afterward. But this was in 2012 and, since then, the tools available for cross-platform development have evolved and the results have improved.

Nowadays, there are a handful of popular cross-platform frameworks, each with their pros and cons. However, native development for each platform is still a very popular choice. The native versus cross-platform dilemma is a controversial topic. We'll see if the dust settles sometime soon.

9

ENCRYPTION

Internet messages travel around the world through wires and Wi-Fi signals. An intruder could easily tap into those channels to snoop into other people's private communication. A really wicked eavesdropper could even alter the content of the intercepted message, causing serious trouble. Communicating through the Internet is as private as writing a message on a post-card: everyone can read it along the way, including the postman, your neighbors and your housemates.

Your business is likely to receive sensitive data from clients over the Internet, such as their credit card numbers or personal ID information. It is also likely to send sensitive data to clients and other businesses, such as invoices and account balances. You wouldn't want any intruders to read those messages. In this chapter, we'll see how online communication is secured and I'll share my advice for keeping you and your customers safe.

ENCRYPTION

If you want to send a message to a friend but keep it a secret, you have to obscure it in a way that only you and your friend know. For example, you could replace every letter in the original message with the next letter in the alphabet. "A" becomes "B," "B" becomes "C," and so on. By using this strategy, the word "hello" is transformed into this apparent nonsense:

ifmmp

A snooper isn't able to understand the actual content of your message. This process is known as *encryption*. Your friend can easily *decrypt* the message by "undoing" the encryption algorithm, replacing every letter by the previous one in the alphabet. "C" becomes "B," "B" becomes "A," and so on.

The problem with this approach is that the secrecy lies in the encryption algorithm itself. Anyone who knows the technique to encode the letters can crack the message.

The solution is to add a password or *key* to the mix. Suppose that, instead of jumping one letter in the alphabet, you use a secret key to indicate how many letters to jump. For example, key "5" means that you skip five letters in the alphabet. The same message is encrypted in different ways depending on the key:

$$\text{hello } + \text{ key 1 } = \text{ifmmp}$$
$$\text{hello } + \text{ key 2 } = \text{jgnnq}$$

Your friend needs to know the value of this key in order to properly apply the decryption algorithm and read the original message. Knowing the encryption algorithm itself is of little value without the key. In fact, everyone could agree on using the same algorithm, but they would make sure that only the intended recipient knows the key. The overall process looks as follows:

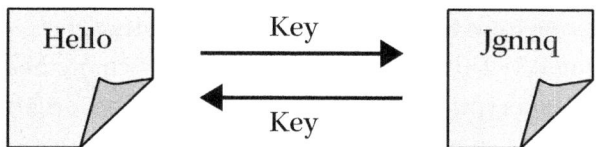

The alphabet algorithm I presented above is very naïve and can be cracked in two distinct ways. First of all, it has design vulnerabilities: it doesn't obfuscate the letters enough. The same letter is always translated the same way in different positions. Therefore, the most frequent letter in the encrypted message is likely to correspond to the most frequently used letter in the English language. If "f" is the letter that appears the most, you can deduce that it was "e" in the original message because "e" is the most popular letter in English. Since "e" became "f," you now know that the key is "1."

Any successful encryption algorithm must mess with the letters much more than that. It should output different symbols for the same character in different positions. Current encryption algorithms perform very complex operations on the input, leaving the message unrecognizable and resistant against any type of linguistics-based analysis.

The second way to crack a code is by brute force, which means trying many keys, one by one, until obtaining a recognizable message. Suppose someone intercepts the message "jbnnq," encrypted by using the alphabet algorithm. The bandit tries to decrypt the message with multiple keys. Key "1" leads to "ifmmp," which is not a recognizable message. But when the bandit tries key "2," the result is "hello," which looks like a real message. The code has been cracked.

Brute-force attacks are prevented by having long keys, which admit many combinations. Encrypted Internet communication uses keys long enough to require millions of times the age of the universe to crack by trial and error. This is more than enough to deter anyone from even trying a brute-force attack.

During WW2, the Germans knew these two ingredients for a successful encryption: significantly altering the original message and doing so with a key with a prohibitive number of combinations to try by hand. They used a machine known as Enigma to encrypt and decrypt messages. This machine looked like a sophisticated typewriter:

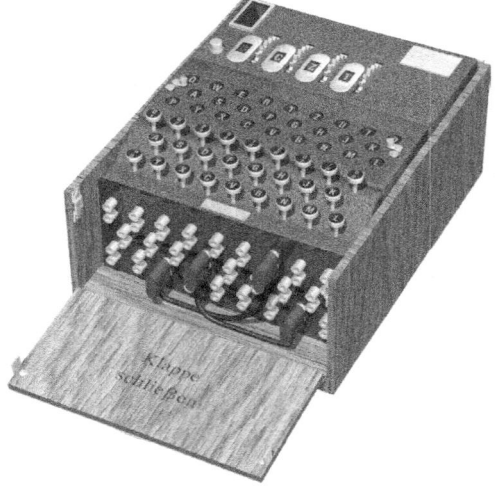

It contained a keyboard to type a message. After pressing a key, a light turned on over another board with the corresponding encrypted or decrypted letter. The internal wiring of the machine implemented the scrambling necessary to obscure the message. This scrambling depended on a secret key, which the operator entered by positioning a few rotating disks, as in a combination lock, and connecting a plugboard in a specific pattern.

To decode a message, the receiver had to have an Enigma machine and configure its disks and plugboard with the right key.

It didn't take long until their enemies stole the design of Enigma and knew exactly how it operated. But the machine in itself wasn't useful without the secret keys. Germans exchanged key books physically through trusted couriers. The keys lasted just one day, and different keys were used in different intelligence departments.

The Polish secretly invented an electro-mechanical device to crack Enigma machine messages. But as the Germans updated Enigma, multiplying the number of possible key combinations, the Polish machine soon became obsolete. The Polish decided to pass on their prototype to the British, who dealt with this in a secret lab in Bletchley Park. In this lab, Alan Turing and Gordon Welchman revisited the idea and took it to the next level.

The first stage of code breaking involved exploiting vulnerabilities to make a good guess about a word in the encrypted text; for example, the Germans often started a message with the word "FORT," which meant that it was a continuation from a previous message (*Fortsetzung*). If an intercepted message started with "PRWF," there were high chances that those letters corresponded to "FORT" because the Enigma machine obfuscated every letter independently but didn't change their order in the text. There was another vulnerability: Enigma machines never encrypted a letter as itself. Therefore, the code breakers could know that "FPQW" would never correspond to "FORT" because an F would never become an F. This helped them prune the set of suspect keywords.

Once the code breakers had a good candidate, such as "PRWF - FORT," they had to find the secret key that made an Enigma machine turn "FORT" into "PRFW." This was done by brute force using *Bombe*, the famous machine invented by Turing and company, trying out many possible secret keys until finding the right one. Once the right key was found, the operators entered it into an Enigma machine by setting up the disks and the plugboard and decrypted the rest of the message. The activities of Bletchley Park were only declassified in 1974.

Contemporary encryption algorithms have overcome the pitfalls of Enigma with a much more obscure scrambling and longer secret keys. They have become, so far, unbreakable.

KEY EXCHANGE

The newest encryption algorithms are good but have a critical weakness: key exchange. Both sender and receiver need to agree on a key in order to read their respective messages. The Germans physically exchanged keys through a courier, but this wouldn't be possible to do between every single pair of computers that communicate securely through the Internet. The trick is to use *asymmetric* encryption, a new type of algorithm invented in the '70s.

Asymmetric encryption uses two keys instead of just one. These two keys are related to each other in such a way that if you encrypt a message with one key, you need the *other* one to decrypt it.

If you generate a pair of keys with this property, you can share one with the world, known as the public key, and keep the other secret, known as the private key. Since the first key is public, everyone can use it to encrypt a message. However, only you can decrypt the message because you're the only person in possession of the private key:

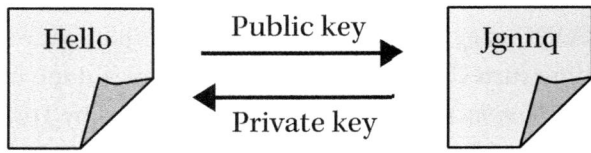

Asymmetric encryption solves the problem of key exchange because there is no need for secrecy: anyone is allowed to know your public key and is able to send you messages that only you can read.

You may be wondering, if you know the public key and the algorithm, why does reversing the algorithm with that key not work to decrypt the message? This is a natural question since most of the mathematical functions we use on a daily basis are easily reversible. For example, you can undo a sum with a subtraction or a multiplication with a division. But asymmetric encryption uses a more complicated function that is hard to reverse.

I'll spare you the mathematical details, but you can think about it this way: Imagine you walk along the shore of a lake a certain distance, say one mile. This distance would be your public key. You could reverse the move by walking one mile in the opposite direction, which would bring you back to the starting position (the original message). But there's a catch: you are only allowed to walk forward along the shore, not backward. Therefore, knowing that the distance walked was one mile is pretty much useless since you can't trace back your steps. You need another, related key that tells you how long to keeping walking to get all the way around the lake to reach the initial spot from behind. Similarly, with asymmetric encryption, due to its mathematical formulation, a message is decoded by encrypting it again the same way but with another, related key that brings you back to the original message.

In the lake example, it is easy to deduce the private key from the public key. You just need to know the length of the lake shore and do the math. But asymmetric encryption is designed in such a way that it is easy to generate a pair of related private and public keys but very hard to find one if you only know the other. For instance, one step in generating the keys involves multiplying two prime numbers, such as 5,003 by 1,229. The result, 6,148,687, can be easily computed and appears as part of the public key for everyone to see. But in order to find the private key, you'd need to find the two numbers whose multiplication gives 6,148,687. This is really hard. You'd have to try thousands of numbers, one by one, until finding the right pair. It is this kind of irreversible mathematical operation that asymmetric encryption is built upon.

DIGITAL SIGNATURES

Asymmetric encryption is also used to sign messages. A digital signature certifies that a message is exactly the one the signee saw. It is used to verify that a message wasn't tampered with.

Digital signatures use a pair of public and private keys but the other way around. Suppose you want to share a signed document. You encrypt it using your private key. The encrypted message can be decrypted by anyone, using the public key. But everyone also knows that you are the only person who could have encrypted that message since only you possess the private key to generate it.

The encrypted message is sent together with the main message and constitutes its digital signature. Everyone can decrypt it with your public key and verify that the result matches the original message. Any tampering with either the message or the signature will result in a mismatch and won't pass the test.

Digital signatures are sometimes used to sign sensitive documents, like police certificates. But, as you'll see in a minute, they have another highly important use.

THE MAN IN THE MIDDLE

If you thought that public and private keys completely solve the problem of key exchange, not so fast. Suppose you ask a website for its public key so that you can send it encrypted messages. An intruder could tap into the line and replace the public key with theirs. You would then be led to believe that you're safely communicating with the website, but someone else is intercepting the messages and decrypting them. The intruder can then encrypt the message with the right public key of the destination and continue sending the message as if nothing had happened. This is known as a man-in-the-middle attack.

A partial solution to this problem is to have someone else certify the veracity of the public key using a digital signature. The certifier should be someone you trust, and the certificate would essentially state, "I assure you that this *really* is the public key you're after."

But, if you remember how digital signatures work, in order to verify a signature, you need to know the signer's public key. An intruder could tamper with that. Therefore, you need someone else to verify the verifier's key... This could go on forever.

The only way to break this "chain of distrust" is if you already know the public key of one of the signers: if you don't have to ask for it then no man in the middle can send you a fake one. When you fully trust the identity of at least one of the signers in the sequence, you can start the encrypted communication. We'll see in a minute how this is handled in the online world.

ENCRYPTION IN PRACTICE

Secure Internet communication is defined in a protocol known as SSL or, more recently, TLS. When you establish a TLS connection with a website, such as facebook.com, the server sends you its public key and a certificate that validates it, signed by another entity. Your Web browser comes with an embedded list of trusted authorities. When Facebook sends you its certificate, the browser checks to see if it's signed by a trusted authority; if it's not, it asks the certifier to provide a certificate of its own identity, issued by someone else. Your browser follows this chain until hitting one of the trusted authorities. Only then will the browser deem that the public key is genuine. Otherwise, it doesn't let you visit the website and shows a red sign saying, "Your connection is not private," which I'm sure you've seen before.

The certification authorities at the top of the chain are a handful of Web giants, including IdenTrust, DigiCert and Go-Daddy. The top five authorities manage 99% of TLS certificates. They follow strict security protocols to issue a certificate, which can go as far as involving notarized signatures and cost from as little as a few hundred dollars a year to thousands. If you want to enable encryption in your own website, you must get a certificate. You can do this through an intermediary, such as your Web hosting provider, who issues a certificate for you and itself is certified by a trusted authority.

Once you confirm the validity of the certificate, you can use Facebook's public key to send them anything you want in complete privacy. This asymmetric encryption is usually only used very briefly. Once you've established the asymmetrically encrypted communication channel, your computer generates its own secret key and sends it to Facebook's server via this secure channel. From then on, you both use that single key in a traditional symmetric encryption algorithm, as in the Enigma machine, because it is much faster.

When you navigate the Web, you'll notice that some addresses start with "https," instead of the old-school "http." This means that TLS is being used and that communication is thus encrypted. An eavesdropper can know who you are communicating with (unless you use a VPN service, as we saw in the Internet chapter), but they can't know what the communication is about. Wikipedia turned on encryption for all its traffic in 2015, arguing that an oppressive government cannot selectively censor pages since they can't know what content the user is reading.

Instant messages, including on WhatsApp and FaceTime, are encrypted end to end, which means that only the two people at the end of the line can decrypt them. No one, including WhatsApp or Apple themselves, can snoop into the messages.

In other cases, the server unencrypts your messages inside its premises, especially when the content needs to be analyzed. This is how Gmail can scan your emails for spam or triage them into the right folders. In the 2013 scandal, National Security Agency documents leaked by Edward Snowden revealed that U.S. government agencies were tapping into Google and Yahoo's private fiber-optic networks, used to connect different servers within the same company. These companies were encrypting communication to and from the Internet but not between their own private servers. In response, the two Internet giants decided to also encrypt all data moved internally.

STAYING SAFE

In the movies, there's always a talented hacker who can penetrate any computer and snoop into any communication. You just need to ask what you want and, in a couple of minutes of typing on a black console with green letters, the hacker infiltrates the CIA's network. This is far from the truth.

Security algorithms are mathematically robust. They don't even need secrecy: everyone knows the details of the algorithms used. Attackers are deterred from using pure brute force since it would take them millions of years to crack the code.

Effective attacks are conducted by exploiting vulnerabilities, which come in all sorts of shapes. For example, attacks can be executed at the physical level by tapping a wire or stealing a hard drive.

Vulnerabilities are also present at the software level. For example, there was a time when a common attack was to enter program code in a form field, such as the "username" box of a login page. If the back-end server embedded the field's input in its program code, the attacker could end up executing intrusive code and stealing data. Nowadays, any well-versed developer is aware of this potential vulnerability and makes sure that user input looks as expected.

Other attacks, known as social engineering, manipulate gullible users. For example, a fake email claiming to be from eBay sends you to a fake eBay website and asks for your credit card details.

Note that while the server's authenticity is validated by a chain of certificates, the user's authenticity is often validated by a much simpler tool: a password. And when people use their birth dates as passwords, it doesn't take too long to crack them. This is another kind of social vulnerability.

For every kind of attack, there is a remedy. Soon after a hacker creatively invents a novel idea to mess with others, the tech community comes up with a countermeasure. A set of best practices has developed in the community and is constantly evolving.

An example is that no reasonable server stores passwords anymore. Until a few years ago, when you registered on a website, they stored your password and even sent you a confirmation email with the password in it. This was prone to all sorts of attacks. Nowadays, your password is stored in an altered way, by using a one-way encryption algorithm. This type of algorithm, known as *hashing*, scrambles the input in a way that is hard to reverse. By looking at the resulting hash code, you can't know which password generated it. When you log in to a website, your password is never used. It is scrambled by using the same algorithm and compared against the stored hash code to see if there's a match. This way, stealing a hard drive proves of little value to an attacker since the hash codes can't be used to log in. Nowadays, when you ask to recover a forgotten password, you receive an email to set up a new one. The server wouldn't be able to send you your password, not even if it wanted to, since it isn't stored anywhere.

Storing a password in a server was common years ago, but now it is one of the cardinal sins of cybersecurity. Two-factor authentication, such as sending an SMS with a code to your phone, seems to be the step forward.

The single best recommendation for staying safe on the Web is to keep up with the advances in cybersecurity. Make sure that your organization knows the state of the art and incorporates the learnings of those who've taken a hit. That is how you outsmart a hacker.

10

BIG DATA

EVERY business must collect data, even if just sales ledgers or clients' contact numbers in a phonebook. In the past, small businesses looking to jump on the digital bandwagon replaced spiral notebooks with Excel spreadsheets. But these days, any business that needs to handle complex records in a robust way needs to move beyond Excel. If you want to get serious about storing data, you need to use a database. We'll see what that is about in a minute.

And still, another wave in data collection is just cresting. In recent years, businesses have started to collect way more data than they need for basic operations. This data, such as a record of user clicks on a website, is used to find patterns and make predictions. The increased amounts of data and its variety have led to a set of new practices, which sometimes contradict the principles behind traditional databases. These new practices are known as *big data*, one of the trendiest buzzwords in the business world today. And no, big data doesn't just mean more data. This chapter will also explore this new paradigm.

DATABASES

A *database* is a fancy name for an organized collection of files. The key to its power is that you do not interact with the data directly. You instead use an intermediary program to manage the underlying data. This program is known as a database management system, or DBMS. Any interaction with the database, such as adding or reading stuff, is done by sending a *query* to the DBMS, which is a text instruction in a special language to tell the DBMS what you want it to do.

The DBMS has built-in mechanisms to guarantee the consistency of the data. For example, suppose that there is a power outage as a passenger is booking a flight. The DBMS guarantees that the database doesn't end up with inconsistent data, such as a partial flight reservation or only the first few digits of the passport number. It allows you to pick up where you left off once the power is back or discard the entire transaction altogether.

A DMBS can also be configured to back up the data automatically, protecting you from hardware failure. It also lets you define who can do what with the data, providing access control. It also guarantees read-after-write consistency: if someone modifies a record, any subsequent reads reflect the updated information. If the DMBS receives a query for a record that is in the process of being updated, it makes the requester wait until the modification finishes.

DBMSs constitute some of the heaviest artillery in the world of software, backed by decades of research and thousands of developers. They range from free open-source software, such as PostgreSQL, to proprietary ones, such as Microsoft SQL Server, IBM DB2 and Oracle, whose licenses are sometimes in the hundreds of thousands of dollars.

QUERYING A DATABASE

Suppose the following table is stored in a database:

Purchases:

Date	Product name	List price	Customer name	Customer phone
Dec 22, 2020	Rubber Duck	$ 15	John Smith	+1 123 456
Dec 23, 2020	Teddy Squirrel	$ 20	Jane Doe	+44 789 987
Dec 24, 2020	Rubber Duck	$ 15	Jane Doe	+44 789 987

This table is used to register purchases from customers, one per row. A lot of business data can be easily tabulated in this way, including sales ledgers, inventory, customer details, passenger records, and so on.

The DBMS takes requests from its users, often over the Internet, to manipulate or read the database. The requests are written in a language known as SQL (pronounced S-Q-L or *sequel*). The following SQL query retrieves the names of clients who bought products for over 17 dollars:

Select `Customer name` from `Purchases` where `List price` > 17

SQL is designed to intuitively match English sentences. The query above asks the DBMS to "select the names of customers from the purchases table where the list price exceeds 17." The DBMS replies as follows:

Customer name
Jane Doe

This is the only row from the table above that matches the criterion in the query.

SQL statements are also used to insert new rows in a table or update existing ones. For example, when Jane Doe bought her rubber duck, the purchase was added to the database by sending the following SQL query to the DBMS:

Insert into Purchases ("Dec 24, 2020", "Rubber Duck", "Jane Doe", "+44 789 987")

These are just a couple of very simple examples, but SQL can be used for sophisticated queries. For example, you can fetch a list with the top 10 products or the highest spending customers. Some DBMSs even let you run geographical queries, such as finding all the customers in a 100-mile radius from a store.

RELATIONAL DATABASES

The *relational* model is a popular way of organizing data, used by almost every DBMS since the 1970s. In a relational database, the data is organized as a series of related tables.

So far, we saw an example of a single table that records all the information known about purchases. But this is a poor way of designing a relational database because there is redundancy in the table. For example, Jane's phone number appears multiple times, for each purchase she's made.

Redundancy is one of the cardinal sins of relational database design. First, it takes space to store repeated values. If Jane had made a thousand purchases, her phone number would appear a thousand times. Second, it takes too much effort to modify redundant data. For example, if Jane changed her phone number, there would possibly be thousands of rows in the purchases table that would need to be modified.

Designing a database involves coming up with an arrangement of tables that avoids redundancy. In the case of the purchases table, this can be achieved by splitting the data into three different tables:

Customers:

Customer number	Name	Phone
#1	John Smith	+1 123 456
#2	Jane Doe	+44 789 987

Products:

Product number	Name	List price
#1	Rubber Duck	$ 15
#2	Teddy Squirrel	$ 20

Purchases:

Date	Customer number	Product number
Dec 22, 2020	#1	#1
Dec 23, 2020	#2	#2
Dec 24, 2020	#2	#1

In this solution, there are dedicated tables to store customer and product information. Jane's phone number, for example, is only recorded once in the customers table. A purchase is registered in a separate table by matching customers and products through their identifiers, telling you something like, "Customer #2 bought product #1 on December 24th." If, at any point, you need to know the phone numbers associated with the purchases, you have to *join* the rows of both tables by matching IDs, which is also done through a special SQL query. The results are combined on the fly, always giving you the most up-to-date phone numbers.

A great feature of a relational DBMS is that it manages the relations between the tables. For example, you can make the DBMS aware that the customer number of a purchase should correspond to an actual identifier from the customers table. The DBMS will then make sure that the consistency of the data is never broken. For example, it prevents you from adding a purchase by a customer that doesn't exist. It also prevents you from deleting a customer that has purchases on record. You can think of a DMBS as a program that not only handles the storage of data but also manages its cross-references.

BIG DATA

Back in the day, businesses only stored the data that was essential to their operations. An online travel agency would only keep track of the flights they sold. Since the advent of predictive analytics, companies now try to store pretty much everything they can with the goal of predicting customer behavior. A travel agency now records every action from users, such as which flights a user saw but chose not to buy. This way, they can understand customer behavior and show relevant results. For example, if customers routinely ignored inconvenient flights with several layovers, they should not be shown at the top of the list. In a similar fashion, Netflix keeps track of the shows you watched, the ones you gave up on and the recommendations you chose to ignore.

There is also an increasing number of sensors that continuously capture new data. I used to write software for a space agency to analyze satellite images. They had a pair of satellites that provided an image of the entire earth every day, at a spatial resolution of less than a meter. If you were sitting with a friend at an outdoor café, there would be a pixel measurement for you, one for your friend, and another one for the guy sitting at the next table. This would go on for the entire surface of the planet, every day.

There are two significant challenges to working with big data. First, the sheer amount of it is really hard to handle using a traditional relational database. A seemingly simple operation, such as joining two tables, can take ages to run if each of your two tables contains millions of rows. Second, the data is often not easily structured in pretty rows and columns. For example, if your data were a collection of news articles fetched from the Web, they would all be of variable length and contain embedded images and other content. A novel paradigm has arisen to cope with the newest needs of the data world.

SCALING HORIZONTALLY

It is tempting to think that the solution to cope with the increased amount of data is to use larger and more powerful computers. But there is no single computer that can provide the power required to process the sheer amount of data companies work with today. The solution is to combine the efforts of multiple computers working simultaneously. This is metaphorically referred to as scaling "horizontally"—essentially like placing many computers side by side. The resulting computers, or *nodes*, are connected to each other via a network, forming a *cluster*.

Instead of storing all the data in a single place, it is split into chunks and distributed across different nodes. This should be done judiciously as moving data from computer to computer can get really slow and congest the network. The trick is to have every computer focus on a subpart of the bigger problem that only involves its own chunk of data. Every node computes a partial solution to the problem and then, at the very end, these partial solutions are collected to give a final result.

Suppose you wanted to find the longest word in a set of news articles collected from the Web. Let's imagine there are millions of articles, stored across 50 different nodes in a cluster. You would solve this problem in two steps. First, each node computes the longest word among the articles it contains. All the nodes compute their own partial results simultaneously, which is much faster than if you were to do a full sweep over all the articles one by one. One node may find that "counterrevolutionaries" is the longest word in its own set of documents, whereas another one may find "internationalization":

After that, one of the nodes collects the partial results and selects the final answer:

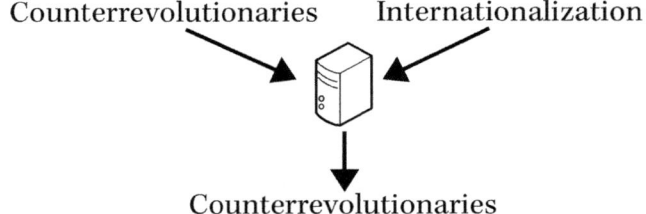

Since the longest of the longest is also the longest overall, this procedure gives the right answer.

Note that the full articles are never exchanged throughout the network. Only the partial results are shared. Since this amounts to only a single word per node, it is fast to do.

Not every problem can be so easily split into parallel tasks.

And the older big data frameworks were quite inflexible: the programmer had to give serious thought about how to break down a problem into steps. There are often different ways of decomposing the same problem, some more efficient than others. But this has changed with more modern frameworks, such as Spark, that are able to analyze your query behind the scenes to automatically create the most optimal execution plan for the task. They even let you formulate queries in the familiar SQL language, as if you were dealing with a traditional relational database. This has made it easier to process big data on a cluster of computers.

Managing big data infrastructure has become so import that it's a specialty in itself, the job of a big data engineer (or just data engineer). They decide how to store and query large data sets, and they prepare and curate the data for others to use.

UNLEARNING RELATIONAL DATABASES

The world of big data has imposed new ways of organizing data, which often contradict the principles that, for decades, ruled relational databases. For example, on a cluster, you want to avoid exchanging data between different nodes as much as possible. But this means certain data must be repeated in multiple nodes, which goes against the old principle of avoiding redundancy.

In big data, redundancy is introduced on purpose to group data that is likely to be used together. It is common to see tables like the following:

Sale date	Product	Customer name	Country	Region
Jan 5, 2020	Rubber Duck	Jane Doe	USA	North America
Jan 7, 2020	Teddy Squirrel	Jane Doe	USA	North America

This is redundant in many ways. First, it contains repeated information about the client for each purchase. In a relational database, this would have been factored out in a separate table. Second, the region (North America) can be easily inferred from the country (USA), so it's unnecessary to record it every time. Why would you want to repeatedly store the name of a region when you can easily deduce it from the country?

The advantage of this redundancy is that a lot of things can be known without needing to visit other tables. You don't need to perform as many expensive join operations so common in relational databases. For example, you can find the region with most sales by looking just at this one table. In a relational database you'd have to access another table to connect a country to a region and compute regional sales numbers.

In big data, redundancy can be a blessing, but it comes with all the complications that gave birth to the relational model in the first place. It is hard to keep the data consistent with so much redundancy in it. You also give up on read-after-write consistency: big data technologies allow users to read content even if someone else's update hasn't finished. This means that others may keep reading outdated data for a while right after you submit a change. This is euphemistically called "eventual consistency" because, at some point in the future, your update will be consistently read by others. Unsurprisingly, there's another phrase I've been hearing a lot lately: "I have data quality issues."

To bring order to chaos, data engineers code data transformations, or ETLs (extract, transform, load). An ETL modifies an existing dataset in a meaningful way and stores the result separately. The modification may involve cleaning the data, showing it in a different way, joining it with other tables, and so on. ETLs are often scheduled to run periodically. For example, every day at midnight, an ETL goes through the newest data from customer activity on your website, reorganizes it and filters it. The morning after, other members of the organization can access the cu-rated dataset.

Big data complements traditional databases rather than replacing them. For anything that requires consistency, such as passenger records and inventory, you're better off using a rela-tional database. If you want to do analytics on a huge dataset, you'll likely need a big data solution.

COLLECTING DATA

My single biggest recommendation for your business is the fol-lowing: collect data. You never know how data may be useful in the future. Storing data has become easier and cheaper than ever, so you have no excuses. If you don't collect data, you may fall behind your competitors who do so.

Nowadays, everyone expects a personalized experience when navigating the Web and that means a data-driven expe-rience. When you visit an online store, you expect to see results sorted by relevance and recommendations tailored to you. If this is not the case, you immediately get a sense of amateurism. You don't want to give your clients that impression. Even if you don't know where your business is going, there is an opportunity cost to running a business and not collecting data. Even if you don't have a use for this data now, you might need it a couple of months or years from now, when you require information about customer behavior to inform some decision.

A good starting point is to keep a record of all your clients' interactions with your Web app. For example, if you run an on-line travel agency, record when a customer has clicked on a flight to know more about it, even if no purchase was made. Also keep track of all the flights you've displayed, and in which order, and how far down the customer scrolled.

You can also keep a log of API transactions with other businesses' Web apps. For example, when you connect to an airline to fetch their inventory, keep track of the prices you were offered for flights. That may be useful for doing stats on flight prices later on. In a nutshell, try to log all the data that has passed through your organization. You may be tempted to dump this data because it isn't directly related to sales, but believe me, in time it may prove useful.

At the same time, you should do this ethically, making sure you're allowed to collect the data, and abide by the highest privacy and security standards and regulations. The topic of regulation is complicated, since every region has its own, but a good idea is to go by the most stringent one. For instance, remember that the EU is quite strict about cookies. Likewise, in 2018, the EU implemented a comprehensive regulation, known as GDPR, that addresses privacy and data protection at a large scale, well beyond cookies. It applies to anyone doing business in Europe, which means that if you're based in the U.S. but have clients in the EU, you must comply with GDPR directives.

One of the requirements of GDPR is that you need individual consent from customers for each use you make of their data. Also, depending on your activity, you may be required to appoint a *data protection officer* in charge of monitoring GDPR compliance. Another requirement is that, when possible, data should be stored in an anonymized way or the names replaced with pseudonyms. This type of storage doesn't harm analytics, where the goal is to find statistical patterns, such as "people who buy A are likely to buy B." You can search for a "GDPR checklist" to assess your standing or simply to have a set of guidelines for data collection.

11

THE CLOUD

THE latest major revolution in the tech world is the cloud. I'm not speaking about you storing your holiday photos in iCloud or Dropbox, even though that is indeed part of the cloud; I'm speaking about *cloud computing*.

Until not so long ago, if your organization needed consequential computing power you had to buy mighty computers and install them in a building known as a data center. Imagine a supermarket, but instead of produce or pantry goods, every shelf and aisle is lined with computers. Data centers need sophisticated mechanisms to keep the air cool and resist power cuts, and the floor is raised to run wires underneath.

A data center required significant upfront costs to set up and significant running costs to maintain. You could rent space in somebody else's data center and put your machines in there, but this was equally inflexible. In case of a surge in demand for your services, such as Christmas shopping in an online store, it was hard to scale the infrastructure. You would need to buy new machines and sign new binding contracts.

But, in 2006, Amazon launched Amazon Web Services, or

AWS, which allows you to dynamically rent computers to run your company's code, and all this can be done over the Internet. Suddenly, companies no longer needed to buy and manage their own computing infrastructure, plus AWS brought access to powerful computers within everyone's reach. We'll see in a bit how this works and how it has changed the tech landscape.

Over the following five years, Google, Microsoft and IBM each opened their own cloud platforms: Google Cloud Platform (GCP), Microsoft Azure and IBM Cloud. Since then, AWS and its competitors have all grown to offer a myriad of cloud services, such as file storage and databases.

CLOUD COMPUTING

In cloud computing, you can rent a computer from the cloud provider in a couple of clicks and then easily send the program code you want to run. This can be used to set up entire Web apps, such as online stores or video streaming platforms. The billing is "pay-as-you-go": you're charged by the time of usage, usually by the minute.

Cloud providers also make it quite easy to scale your operation. If there is a surge in demand, you can simply rent more computers with a couple of clicks and release them when they are not needed. You can also configure this to scale automatically: you can tell your provider to hire and release computers automatically to meet the demand from users. You can also rent a super powerful computer that you would never want to buy yourself for a one-time processing boost.

Cloud providers have installed data centers all over the world, organized by region. For example, AWS runs independent data centers in multiple regions of the U.S., Ireland, Singapore, and many other locations around the world. Each region contains multiple *availability zones*, which are areas far enough from each other to avoid being exposed to the same hazards. For example, if a tornado hits one availability zone, it is very unlikely to affect another zone.

If you want to deploy a robust Web application, you must hire computers in at least two different zones. A so-called load balancer distributes the requests from users among the different available computers. If one of the zones suffers from an outage, the load balancer automatically sends all the requests to the other, surviving zone.

You should also choose convenient locations to minimize the delays in moving data. For example, if your clients are mostly in Europe, you would want to run your Web app in machines located nearby. I once worked with a client that needed to perform very fast calculations in an area of the earth underserved by cloud providers. The closest data center was 6,000 miles away, and the time to bring the results back home was too long and unacceptable for the application. This company ended up buying their own servers for faster processing. However, it didn't take long until one of the cloud giants installed data centers nearby.

Renting a respectable computer and using it to run usual business operations 24 hours a day, 7 days a week, would cost you around $1,700 a year. Renting a powerful computer, with 96 cores and 384 GiB of memory, would cost north of $35,000. But you usually only need that kind of power for sporadic processing, such as training machine learning models and doing analytics, which doesn't require to run constantly. Once you're done with the task, you simply release the computer and stop paying for that time. If you used that powerful machine only four hours a day, it would take you at least a couple of years until the cloud bill exceeded the cost of buying your own machine. And this is without considering the cost of maintaining the infrastructure or the opportunity cost of being stuck with the machine you bought and having to pay more to change or upgrade it.

CLOUD STORAGE

By hiring a computer when you need it and then releasing it when you're done, anything you may have saved in it gets lost. Therefore, cloud providers offer an independent set of clever solutions to persistently store files in the cloud. For example, AWS offers a storage service called S3. When you drop a file in S3, it is automatically copied in different zones, protecting it from all kinds of hazards. Its creators have designed it to lose one file every ten million years. No file has ever been lost yet.

Storage is billed by the size of the data and the number of times it is accessed or modified. For example, storing one terabyte of data (300 hours of HD video) on S3 would cost you $280 dollars per year, assuming files are read a million times a month. Storing the entire Wikipedia, with all its images (200 terabytes), would cost you $60,000 a year.

Cheaper alternatives are also available. For example, if you don't mind storing your files in just one zone, that would cut your bill in half. But in the unlikely event of a complete destruction of the zone, you would lose your files. It's up to you. Also, if you don't mind waiting a while to retrieve the files, you can use a cheaper but slower service and cut down the bill by five times. This would be appropriate, for example, for an infrequently accessed archive.

Even with the fastest storage options, there is a slight delay when a file is accessed from overseas. The data needs to travel a long distance through the Internet. Therefore, cloud providers offer smart services to store additional copies of the most frequently accessed files in several places over the earth. For example, suppose your website's images are stored in S3, in Ireland. The first time someone from Japan visits the website, the content travels across the continents. But a copy of the image is stored temporarily somewhere along the way, for example, in India. The next time someone from Japan, Singapore or Australia requests that file, it is fetched from India instead of Ireland, reducing the travel time. This temporary storage only holds a fraction of the original data and removes infrequently accessed files, making it a cost-effective way to speed up the retrieval of your most popular content.

SERVERLESS COMPUTING

One of the most disruptive cloud innovations came in 2014, almost a decade after the beginning of cloud computing. Up until that point, running a program on the cloud involved renting the machine, setting it up, sending the program code, executing it, and releasing the infrastructure when you were finished.

With *serverless* computing, you simply ask the cloud provider to execute a program for you and they automatically handle the rest. You don't need to reserve or set up a dedicated machine; you simply give the cloud provider your code and a set of directions for when to execute it. For example, suppose every time a user uploads an image, you would like to resize it. Through your cloud provider's management console, you connect the event of uploading a file to the piece of program code that resizes the image. On the upload of a new image, the cloud provider allocates some of the resources available at the time to execute the program.

Serverless computing is not really serverless; you simply can't see the server because it is running under the hood. But it spares you the trouble of maintaining the server. You don't have to worry about renting a machine, setting it up and releasing it, and you don't pay for any idle time. You are billed per 0.1 seconds of processing time your program used. But you need to do the math because sometimes serverless computing can be more expensive than setting up a server in the traditional way.

TO CLOUD OR NOT TO CLOUD

What I've mentioned so far is just the tip of the iceberg. Cloud providers are offering an ever-growing list of services for all sorts of things. The question is: should you use your own computing infrastructure or put your business in the cloud?

Having your own computers is known as working "on-premises" because they are installed inside the premises of your organization. This is rarely the best choice for small or medium companies. The cloud gives you the flexibility you need at a fraction of the cost. You can even pretend that your start-up is a giant, running experiments on super powerful machines you wouldn't be able to afford otherwise. Cloud computing has brought the power of innovation within everyone's reach.

Even the largest companies are progressively migrating to the cloud, abandoning their old, on-premises infrastructure. There was some resistance at first, but most have taken the leap. Some of the resistance came from concerns about storing sensitive data off-site or the cost involved in the migration itself.

And it is true that, over time, the cloud bills start to add up. There is a balance point at which it becomes more cost effective to have your own on-premises infrastructure. For example, Dropbox migrated *out* of the cloud in 2016 and moved its operations into its own data centers. But it has 500 million users and, after all, it specializes in storage solutions.

But for most businesses, the cloud has given rise to a new way of thinking about computing. Cloud computing offers an easy, cost-saving option for many Web apps, but you do need to manage your cloud usage judiciously. It is easy to spend too much accidentally by hiring a machine that is more powerful than needed or even by forgetting to release the infrastructure you're not using.

DEVELOPING SOFTWARE FOR THE CLOUD

The advent of cloud computing gave rise to a new profession: the cloud engineer, in charge of planning and managing all things related to the cloud.

With everything being delocalized, engineers think about the travel time, or *latency*, needed to communicate data between remote cloud servers. Even though the cloud sounds like something up in the sky, the engineers are always well aware of the geographical locations of the servers—or what is roughly known about their locations since the actual coordinates are usually a trade secret.

Most software developers now use their laptops as mere windows to visualize what's happening in the remote cloud computers. They may write code locally in their own machines, but they send it to the cloud for execution. Therefore, it has become less and less important to have a powerful computer to write software. A few years ago, my work laptop was so heavy it kept ripping my backpack. I had the best computer you could fit into the size of a (large) laptop because I constantly had to run complicated software. The company I worked for had its own on-premises data center with powerful computers, but they were often hogged by someone else, so I still needed a good laptop to get anything done. This has certainly changed with cloud computing. These days, little happens in my computer anymore. One of my colleagues recently exchanged her sleek MacBook Pro for an even sleeker MacBook Air because she found it easier to carry around. But behind the scenes, she is running very complicated software in the secret innards of a cloud data center.

PART III

ARTIFICIAL INTELLIGENCE

12

MACHINE LEARNING

I F you search the term *artificial intelligence*, you are likely to find circular definitions: it is "intelligence demonstrated by machines" or "the simulation of human intelligence." I like to follow a more pragmatic definition: artificial intelligence seeks to solve problems for which we cannot easily imagine an algorithm (a list of steps).

For example, what is the algorithm to detect if a tweet expresses a positive or negative sentiment? One idea is to count how many words in a tweet are positive, such as "best" or "nice," and compare this with the number of negative words, such as "ugly" or "ugh." However, this is problematic with ironic tweets, where positive words are used in a negative sense and vice versa. There is no straightforward list of steps to solve this problem.

Another example is machine translation. Is there an algorithm, a specific list of steps, to flawlessly translate sentences? I recently saw a Facebook post where someone complained about being "tired of tails." It turns out that this person was tired of standing in line, but in the post's original language, Spanish, "queue" and "tail" are the same word. Problems like these go beyond the ones with well-known mechanical solutions, such as multiplying or sorting numbers, and thus belong in the realm of artificial intelligence.

An old approach to artificial intelligence is to write a list of rules that mimic human decisions. For example, suppose an online store wants to show a recommendation for another product after a client makes a purchase. A programmer could do this by writing rules; for example, "suggest a gym mat to any customer who purchases a dumbbell," or, "suggest coffee grains to anyone who buys a coffee machine." While this does count as artificial intelligence, it is pretty rudimentary. A far more powerful kind of artificial intelligence has made the headlines in recent times: *machine learning*.

With machine learning, instead of writing absolutely every detail of an algorithm, its creator leaves some moving parts, which can be configured in different ways. The best configuration for these moving parts is determined automatically from patterns detected in data. The process by which the machine decides how to configure the moving parts is known as *learning*, and the data used to make that decision is known as *training data*.

Machine learning is omnipresent in your daily life. Every time you use a product that would require a long list of rules being written to create it, it is very likely it was done with machine learning instead. For example, when you search something, Google often provides additional results for other related search terms. But the list of related terms was probably learned from data. For example, the fact that "Big Apple," "Manhattan" and "New York City" are related search terms is probably learned from webpage content or records of past user searches, instead of written by hand. (I don't know this for a fact, since I wasn't involved in building it, but I would bet on it.) Imagine how cumbersome it would be to write the myriad of rules that associate the thousands of possible search terms. Similarly, any recommendations or targeted ads arise from machine learning. There's no one writing individual rules that say that if you liked *Forrest Gump* you'd enjoy *The Terminal*. Machine learning is also used to analyze signals, like images and speech, to perform tasks like detecting objects, recognizing faces and transcribing speech.

The huge potential of machine learning has garnered it significant attention from media and investors, but it is still one of the less understood technologies. In this chapter, I'll walk you through the components of a machine learning solution. The next few chapters will discuss other aspects of machine learning, such as how to make sure that whatever the machine learns makes sense.

THE PROBLEM

Let's assume you and your friends have founded Flixnet, a totally original streaming platform to watch movies at home. You decide to give a one-month free trial period to your clients. Your goal is to predict which clients will keep your service after the trial period and which will leave. If you can predict which clients are likely to leave, you can take action to retain them, such as sending them an email announcing the imminent release of new shows.

This is the first ingredient to the mix: a problem. Quite often, problems are formulated as *classification*: the need to assign each item to a category. In the case of Flixnet, you want to predict if a customer belongs to the *stay* class or *leave* class.

In other cases, problems are formulated as *regression*, which means you want to predict a specific value, such as a train's estimated delay in minutes.

THE DATA

Machine learning models need training data to learn from, and sometimes a lot of it. This data tends to come from past experience, with known results. At Flixnet, for example, you should keep a record of the outcome after the trial period for past customers, together with general data about them, such as age and location. If you do this for a year or so, you will collect a sizable amount of data to learn patterns from, known as your *dataset*.

In Flixnet's dataset, you know the "truth" for each of the past clients—did they stay or leave?—so the dataset is already *labeled*. In this case, the labeling is done automatically; you only needed to keep track of which users left and which stayed. But in other cases, humans have to label the past data by hand, sometimes for tens of thousands of instances. For example, for the problem of classifying images into categories, human observers manually browse and label thousands of images into the right categories. A popular and publicly shared dataset for this task is ImageNet, which contains 14 million images that have been humanly labeled into 20,000 categories, such as "dog" and "strawberry." Researchers use this dataset to build algorithms that automatically classify images into their respective ImageNet categories.

Let's assume you've already spent some time collecting data at Flixnet. A schematic representation of the resulting dataset is as follows:

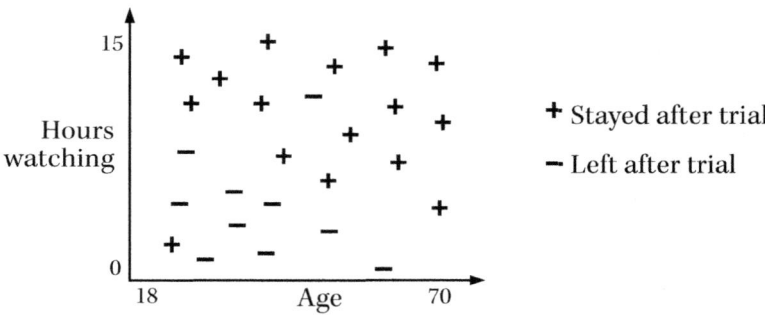

Each plus sign represents a past client who stayed and each minus sign a client who left after the one-month trial. The two axes depict two additional things you know about the clients: their age and how many hours they spent watching Flixnet during the free trial period. These two additional aspects seem to be good predictors of behavior: the older the clients and the more time they watch TV, the more likely they are to stay.

These known characteristics about each client are known as *features*. Your goal is to find patterns that predict customer behavior based on the values of those features. Our example contains only two features (age and hours watching), but it is quite common to work with hundreds if not thousands of them. This may sound crazy, but think of all the things you know about your customers. You know their age, location, language, browsing patterns, ratings, operating system, and so on. You can reach one hundred features quite easily.

From all the available features, you need to carefully choose which ones to include in the model. Having too many features can be problematic and hard to cope with, but too few can make your data too simplistic to learn predictive patterns from it. Feature selection can be a tedious process, sometimes performed by hand and with knowledge of the business field.

Some potential features are completely uninformative and should be left out. For example, let's imagine you identify your customers by a random numeric ID, such as "Client #1575." While it is tempting to put any data you have in your dataset, it would be a poor choice to include the ID because it is not predictive of customer behavior. In fact, most clients don't even know their own IDs, let alone use them in the decision of whether to keep Flixnet. If you put the ID in the dataset, you are giving the machine learning algorithm the opportunity to find a pattern based on it, even though you know that such a pattern cannot exist. As we'll see later on, finding bogus patterns is a real possibility and concern, so you're better off not including data like the ID at all. I've seen this as a trick question in job interviews. The candidates are given some data to process, with a random ID number in it, to see if they effectively exclude the ID from the analysis.

In addition to carefully selecting existing features, you may want to create new ones, which is known as *feature engineering*. For example, you could create a continent feature, derived from the country, if you suspect that clients from the same continent share common purchase patterns.

There are also many technical aspects to consider when selecting and engineering features; for example, including two features that are correlated with each other may hinder the learning process. As you can see, feature selection and engineering is an art and a science.

THE MODEL

A model seeks to convey the relationship between the features (age, time spent watching) and the target variable (stay/leave). Once you've created a model with past data, you will reuse it to predict the behavior of future clients. Let's have a look at two potential models for Flixnet's dataset, side by side:

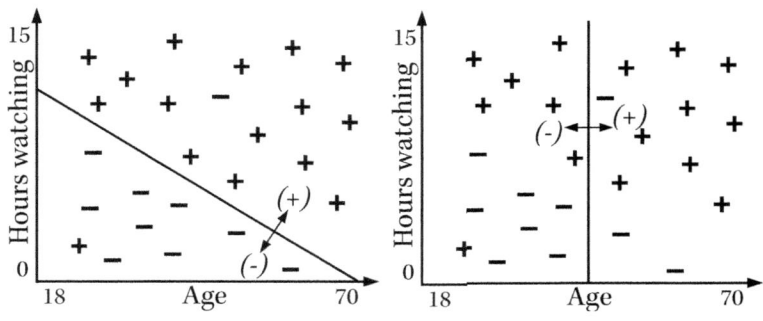

These models use a straight line to divide the clients into those who stay and those who leave: one side of the line is considered to be the plus side and the other one the minus side. When new customers are at the end of their trial periods, you use their features (age and hours watching) to see on which side of the line they fall. If they fall on the positive side, you predict they will stay beyond the trial period, but if they fall on the negative side you predict they will abandon Flixnet.

The model on the left is good at explaining the data because it only places two points on the wrong side of the line. The model on the right, however, is pretty bad; it doesn't capture the underlying pattern. This is what machine learning is used for: you use a program to choose the best model based on how well it fits the data. Hopefully, in this case, the program will choose the left-hand model, which is much better at describing the above dataset.

But not everything is learned from data: you always need to give some fixed structure to your models. In the example above, the fixed structure is that the model takes the shape of a straight line, separating pluses from minuses. The structure imposed may or may not be appropriate, depending on the problem. In that example, a straight line conveniently works, but this is not always the case. For instance, in a different dataset the pluses may be concentrated inside a circular area and the minuses outside that area.

Once the fixed structure is defined, you are left with the moving parts of the model, known as *parameters*, which are not defined in advance. In the example above, the parameters are the specific coordinates of the straight line. The learning process involves looking at the dataset to find the coordinates of the best fitting line. In other words, the model's designer has decided that the model looks like a straight line but leaves it up to the machine learning algorithm to choose which straight line it is. This model only has two parameters because a straight line in 2-D is described by two numbers. But sophisticated models that seek to convey complex patterns often have tens of thousands of parameters.

The model structure comes in many possible shapes. A straight line is just one of them. The designer of a model needs to choose which structure is most relevant to the problem. Another example of model structure is decision trees, which use a cascade of if-then decisions, such as "if age < 35," to give a final classification verdict. The fixed part of the model is the fact that you use a tree to make decisions, and the learnable parameters are which decision to include in each branch of the tree. Another popular type of model, known as random forest, combines the decisions of multiple trees. There is a myriad of model types to choose from, each with their pros and cons.

THE COST FUNCTION

When I showed you the two different models before, side by side, it was quite clear that one model was superior to the other. This is obvious to the human eye, especially in that simplistic 2-D dataset—but that is not how computers work. A computer can't just eyeball it. If you want an algorithm to find the best model, you need to convey the notion of model superiority in a computational way. This is done by writing a mathematical function that measures the quality of the model.

In the Flixnet example, a way to do this would be to count how many points are on the wrong side of the line. If you go back to the figure above, you'll see that the left side model assigns only two points to the wrong category, while the other one misclassifies nine. This metric is known as cost function, energy function, loss function or error, and you wish to find the model with the lowest value.

While counting points is a good approximation, it is not entirely satisfactory because many different lines are equally good, as in the following example:

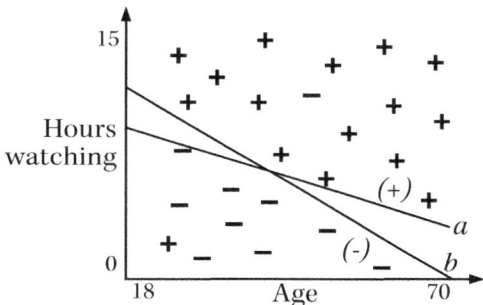

Here both lines exhibit a cost of 2 because both place two points on the wrong side of the line. However, one of the lines is a bit too close to some of the points (line a), while the other one leaves a higher margin of safety (line b). The designer of the cost function would add a term to favor the model with the highest margin. This is just one example of what it entails to design a cost function. Having the right cost function is fundamental to the success of your method.

THE OPTIMIZATION ALGORITHM

You have chosen a straight-line model for Flixnet and an adequate cost function to measure how well the model fits the data. The missing bit is to find which of all possible lines is the best, according to that cost function. In technical terms, you want to find the parameter values (the coordinates of the line) that minimize the cost (the amount of error).

A computer has no clue about this, not even where to start. As a human, you visualize where the line should be to split the pluses from the minuses, which makes it seem easy. But computers need a list of steps to solve a problem. Moreover, your intuition works well in 2-D but can't take you too far with more features. If you have three features, you can imagine that they form a cube, which you split with a razor blade instead of a line. But you won't be able to visualize the problem that easily in 4-D or more.

You need an organized process, an algorithm, to find the parameters that give the best line. This is when *optimization algorithms* come to the rescue. These are algorithms that try out many different parameter values in an organized manner to try to find the best ones (the ones that give the lowest cost). They are designed to explore candidate values in a clever way, trying to avoid spending too much time exploring ranges of values that are unlikely to give good results.

Optimization algorithms are used outside machine learning as well. For example, suppose an airline needs to assign crew members to flights. There are many ways of doing that, some more efficient than others. For example, the more the crew has to stay overnight at a destination the more the airline has to spend in crew accommodation. But you can't always fly them home immediately, due to the rest period required between flights. Optimization algorithms are routinely used by airlines to find crew schedules that minimize the cost while meeting the regulations.

In the case of Flixnet's straight-line model, a naïve optimization algorithm is to randomly try many straight lines and select the one with the lowest cost. This brute-force approach isn't very effective, especially when you have thousands of parameters instead of the two of the straight line. It would take too long to hit on a good solution. A more efficient approach is to start with a random line and tweak it a little in different directions to see what happens. You then move the line slightly in the direction that seems the most promising. This process is repeated again and again. You stop when you find out that tweaking the line in any direction leads to worse solutions than the one you already have. This is similar to how ophthalmologists test a patient's vision to fit a glasses prescription. They change the lens slightly, making it weaker or stronger with each tweak, and ask the patient if the letters on the vision chart look clearer or blurrier. When the patient's vision gets worse with tweaks in any direction, they know they've hit the best prescription.

This optimization algorithm is known as *gradient descent* and is the most popular one in machine learning.

One of the curses of gradient descent is that taking baby steps toward better solutions can get you stuck in a bad one. Consider the following example:

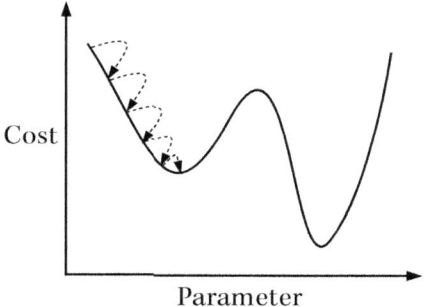

This figure illustrates the cost for different values of a single parameter. You want to find the lowest point of the curve. Looking at the entire graph as a whole is cheating because in real life you can't know in advance the cost associated with each possible parameter unless you try.

The gradient descent starts from a random value. In this case, we assume it starts at the top left corner of the figure. The algorithm then takes baby steps in the direction that lowers the cost, as shown by the dotted arrows in the figure. When it finds that neither moving forward nor backward can lower the cost anymore, it stops. But this gets you stuck in a bad valley. It appears to be the best solution when you look around, but it's not. If you were willing to move to a bad solution first, by climbing uphill to the right, you would then go down on the other side of the hill and find a better valley. But you can't know this unless you try. There are several strategies to escape bad valleys and find good solutions, but they usually can't guarantee to find the best one.

Optimization algorithms tend to have several adjustable settings that determine their behavior, like the length of the steps in the gradient descent or where to start the descent. Sometimes it takes several attempts to hit the right settings to obtain a good solution.

If the problem is easy enough, the optimization algorithm may run quite fast, maybe in less than a second. But, for example, in deep learning, which we will address in the next chapter, entire days if not weeks are often spent running an optimizer to find the best parameters. This is what people mean when they say they are *training* a model.

GOING LIVE

Training a model can take a long time. Once this process is over, using the resulting model is much faster. For example, with Flixnet, it could take a while to find which straight line is the best to split the dataset into two categories. However, once this line is known, it is lightning fast to make predictions about new clients by checking on which side of it they fall.

This is also true with more sophisticated algorithms, such as deep learning. It may take days to find the right set of parameters to configure the model, but then it only takes a few milliseconds to compute a prediction. This has been made even faster by using graphics cards (GPUs), which are powerful processing units that are now embedded even in smartphones.

Think of an iPhone's Face ID, which recognizes the user's face to unlock the phone. This feature took months to develop, including training sophisticated machine learning algorithms. Now that the program has been configured, it verifies the owner's identity in a fraction of a second.

THE PEOPLE OF MACHINE LEARNING

Data scientists are the professionals in charge of creating machine learning models. They formulate the problem, select and engineer features, choose a model type, select a cost function, and run an optimization algorithm. They use the data produced and curated before by a *data engineer* (a.k.a. big data engineer), and the two specialties may sometimes overlap.

The work of a data scientist is at the crossroads between computer science, mathematics and statistics. Quite often, a recruiter searches for a mathematical kind of person and not necessarily a software developer. It is common for other professionals, such as physicists and engineers, to convert into data science. In the field of investment, they are known as *quants*, short for quantitative analysts. They develop machine learning models for trading assets.

Data scientists use friendly software tools that make their work easier. For example, they write their code in a web-based editor, known as a *notebook*, which lets them plot graphs and selectively run small snippets of code, possibly out of order. This lets them experiment with the data and different models in an agile way. Notebooks give the data scientist creative freedom, but the resulting prototype is hardly ever ready to be deployed in a production system used by real clients.

A *machine learning engineer*, or quant developer in investment, is a software developer who specializes in converting or "productionizing" these experimental models into operational ones. This may involve rewriting the model in a different programming language or optimizing it to run faster. I used to work for an online travel agency that used machine learning models in real time to service clients' requests. Over 20 million predictions were made per minute. The models created by data scientists were mathematically sound and good at making predictions but couldn't handle that workload. They had to be reengineered and sped up to go into production successfully.

WILL MACHINE LEARNING WORK FOR YOU?

Most machine learning applications are based on the blueprint I shared with you in this chapter. If you have an idea you think could benefit from AI, you can use this blueprint to imagine what the solution would look like.

For example, suppose you work at a bank and want to predict if a card transaction is fraudulent so that you can take action immediately. You have historical data of past transactions with descriptive features like the amount of the transaction, the timestamp, the location, and the product bought. The data scientist in charge of building the model may even engineer new derived features from that information. For each past transaction, you also know whether it was reported as fraudulent or not (the true label). This is your dataset.

The data scientist will choose a type of model, probably something like a decision tree since a simple straight line can be a bit limiting. Afterward, he or she will define a cost function to quantify the error and use an optimization algorithm to find the model that best fits the data. And there you have a machine learning model.

Or imagine you work for a ski resort and you're not satisfied with the ordinary weather forecast, which tells you it will snow heavily in the next 24 hours but not exactly how much. You want to know a precise value in inches. The mountain is equipped with sensors that measure pressure, temperature, wind and other weather variables. And you have a historical record of these past measurements (the features) and how much it snowed the day after they were taken (the true label). There's your dataset. It is then used by a data scientist to train a model that predicts snowfall in inches from weather measurements following the principles we've seen. I'm not saying this will work. Maybe the inches are hard to predict from the measurements you have, or they are hard to predict in general. But you get the gist.

I recently spoke with a data scientist who was building a machine learning model for a hospital to predict if a walk-in patient was likely to be infected with COVID-19 based on the symptoms displayed. This was being built to assist the triage process, not to make any medical decisions (but the data scientist was a bit concerned about the ethical implications of his work). By now, you can probably guess how the machine learning model was built. There was a dataset of past patients with a list of features describing their symptoms. Each record was paired with the result of a COVID-19 test, indicating whether the patient was infected. You've already heard the rest of the story: model, cost function, optimization. Despite only having a couple thousand patient records in the dataset, the resulting model was quite predictive (which shows that a huge dataset is not always required).

You may have an idea for a business based on AI, or you may want to use AI to improve a process within an existing business. In addition to thinking about the machine learning blueprint from this chapter, I suggest you ask yourself two fundamental questions:

1. *Are you trying to find a pattern that really exists?*

Suppose you want to create an algorithm that detects if someone is lying in a text message. But is there an actual pattern to that in the first place? Are there identifiable ways of recognizing lies in text? I don't know. It's not my field of expertise. But I doubt it.

Some people have the fantasy that machine learning can easily solve any problem. "Just use AI to do it," they say. But AI won't magically help you if there's no pattern to be found.

Compare that to the task of this chapter: predicting the behavior of Flixnet's customers. It's easy to imagine that customer characteristics, such as demographics, are good indicators of behavior. Patterns certainly exist.

2.   *Can you get the data for it?*

Even if a pattern likely does exist, do you have the data required to train a model to find it? Think about it: the lie detector would need thousands of labeled samples of truth and lies in text in order to even try to find predictive patterns from it. That doesn't seem to me like the easiest data to collect.

If you don't have the data, you may be able to acquire it or adapt other, related data to your problem. But the more indirect steps to get the data you want, the harder and less reliable it all gets.

If you've answered yes to both these questions, you're in a good position to use machine learning. There are still many challenges you might face. It may be hard to find patterns if they are too complex or if the data is cluttered. But if you are confident that a pattern does exist and that you have the dataset to find it, you've at least avoided some of the most common pitfalls of machine learning.

13

PREDICTIONS THAT MATTER

How can you make sure that machine learning finds meaningful patterns as opposed to bogus ones? Sadly, training a machine learning model only to have it make nonsensical predictions is more common than you think. And it often goes unnoticed. Believe me; you don't want your business to be basing decisions on the bogus predictions of a mistaken model.

In this chapter, I'll show you several ways in which machine learning can go wrong as well as the techniques to *validate* a model—that is, to make sure it does what it is intended to do. The validation of models is the most important thing that a non-techie involved in machine learning should learn because it is how a business can give a verdict on the quality of a model and how an error can be caught early on.

OVERFITTING AND UNDERFITTING

Let's return to this Flixnet dataset from before:

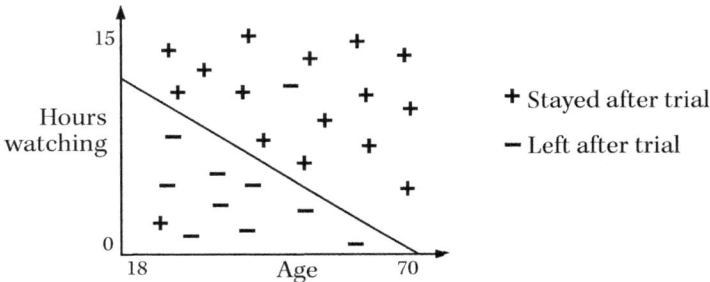

It records the actions of past customers: if they kept (+) or left (-) your movie streaming service after the end of the trial period, depending on their age and the number of hours they spent streaming video.

The straight line cutting the graph in two halves is the model. It is the line that best discriminates the pluses from the minuses in the historical data. New clients are predicted to stay or leave based on which side of the line they fall to.

This model is almost perfect on the historical data, except that it places two past customers on the wrong side of the line:

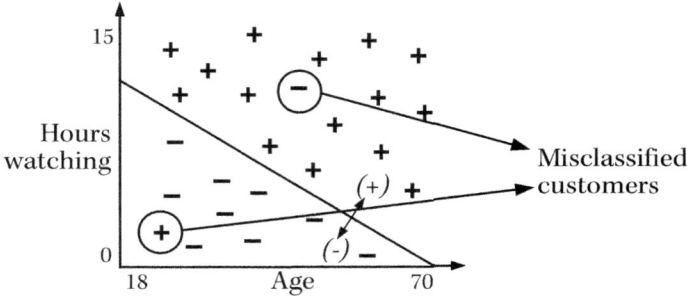

You could improve the model by increasing its complexity, allowing more sophisticated shapes than a basic straight line:

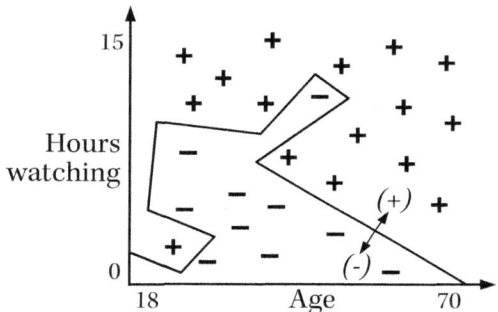

This model has 100% performance on past data. It places every single customer on the appropriate side of the jagged line. It is really good at predicting ... the past.

For any dataset, you can always increase the model complexity until it explains the dataset perfectly. But this doesn't mean that the pattern your insanely complex model found makes any sense.

The zigzag model above forced itself around the individual data points instead of capturing the real forces that drive customer behavior. The old straight line discovered a real pattern: older clients and those who spend more time streaming video are more likely to stay. But the more complex model adapts excessively to specific past training cases instead of learning real insight about the customers.

This is like preparing for a test in school. You could memorize the answers to all the questions asked by the teacher in previous exams. Your performance would be 100% on them. However, you wouldn't learn the concepts required to pass the subject. When you sat the exam and the teacher asked new questions that you hadn't ever seen before, you would fail.

The goal of a machine learning model is to predict *unseen* data—that is data that wasn't used to construct the model.

Therefore, the performance of a model must be measured on a different dataset, independent from the training set. For this reason, a data scientist always excludes a portion of the available data, acting as if it didn't exist, and uses it later on to validate that the model is really capable of predicting things. Otherwise, it is easy to cheat.

The separate data used to evaluate a model is known as a *hold-out* or *test set*. It should ideally be kept in a secret vault until the very end, when the final models proposed by data scientists are evaluated. For example, the online community Kaggle organizes machine learning contests, in which participants create models using a dataset and submit their predictions. The contest organizers provide the dataset but don't release the test data until after the submission deadline. They select a winner by measuring the performance of each prediction on their hidden, labeled test set. A model that is good on unseen data is said to *generalize* well. The predictive model that generalizes the best wins the prize.

The zigzag model above would win no prizes because it would perform badly on unseen data. The line has a protruding blob and aggressive zigzags just to account for two specific, deviant cases in the data. These were likely exceptions to general customer behavior and will not appear again in the future. A simple straight line is more future-proof since it conveys an actual pattern of behavior.

The typical relationship between the predictive performance of a model and its complexity is as follows:

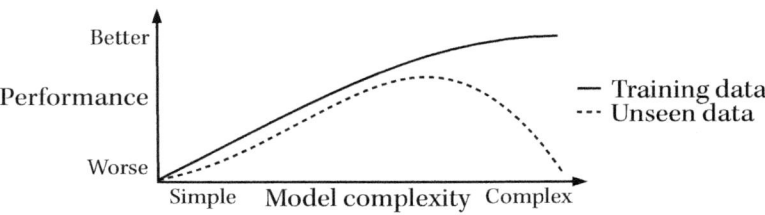

When the model is very complex, as in the right-hand side of this graph, the performance looks great on the data used to train the model, but it collapses on unseen data. This problem, known as *overfitting*, is the bane of a data scientist's existence. It is easy to be fooled into believing that a model has learned, while it has only memorized spurious correlations.

You don't want an overly simple model either, as in the left of the figure, because the predictive performance is also unsatisfactory. This is known as *underfitting* because the model lacks the complexity required to fit the data in a meaningful way. Data scientists experiment with several models, hoping to find the one in the sweet spot of that graph where the performance on unseen data is best.

THE TEST SET PARADOX

Using a test set to measure predictive performance is somewhat paradoxical. A model could do well simply by chance. Suppose I ask you to create a model to predict the result of flipping a coin ten times. I will evaluate all your proposed models on a secret sequence of ten random tosses, only revealed at the very end. But since tossing a coin is completely random, no model should really predict it.

Suppose that you create a thousand different candidate models, which predict coin tosses from the weather or the stock market. None of them is, of course, true. However, there are 98% chances that one model will predict the exact test sequence, just by chance. You and I could end up believing that the model is capable of predicting random coin tosses. The more models you compare and the smaller the test set, the more you can be fooled by randomness.

Ideally, a test set should be used just once, to give a final verdict on a model before productionizing it. If you use the test set to compare different models, discard the bad ones, and refine the best ones, then the test set becomes part of your training data because you're using it as feedback to construct the model.

Knowing this risk, the testing procedure of an organization must be designed with care. The best way to do it is to have a large test set and to only compare a few preferred models. The test set should be used only once. New test rounds should be conducted on newly collected data.

Companies implement this process more or less meticulously, depending on their needs. A hedge fund could lose millions by trading with a bogus model. Netflix will survive if the model that recommends TV series isn't the best. It's up to you. Sadly, a lot of companies aren't even aware that their testing procedures are not as rigorous as they think they are. They often only catch the error when using a model with real clients.

I once joined a company that had been using a flawed testing procedure for nearly two years. The alleged positive results had caught the attention of the company's management, which decided to allocate a greater budget to expand this successful project. This led to several new hires, including me. We discovered the glitch a few months later. It was an awkward situation because several jobs had been opened based on botched results. We took the bull by the horns and decided to fix the broken validation process and rerun the experiments from scratch. The results weren't as good as before, but, fortunately, they were still good enough. We were lucky. It could have been much, much worse, as far as botched machine learning models go.

THE VALIDATION SET

If data scientists can't look at the test data, how can they know if their models make any sense before the final test round? Or how can they search for the sweet spot between overfitting and underfitting? The trick is to hold out an additional portion of the available data, which acts as a pretend test set. This is known as the *validation set*. Altogether, the data needed to train, validate, and test a machine learning model should be broken up something like this:

Training data		Test data (10%)
Training set (80%)	Validation set (10%)	

The models are trained by using the reduced training set. The validation set is then used to measure the performance and select the best models among several candidates. This seeks to simulate what would happen when the final, unseen, test set is revealed.

It is also common to do cross-validation, in which different portions of the training data take turns being the validation set and the resulting measurements are averaged. But since the validation set in this scenario is used repeatedly to refine the models, it does not constitute a clean, "snoop-free" measurement. The real verdict always comes afterward, from the unseen test set.

DATA LEAKAGE

Sometimes data that isn't supposed to be used for training finds its way into the training set by accident. This is known as *data leakage*.

Let's have a look at a stock chart, which records the daily price of a stock:

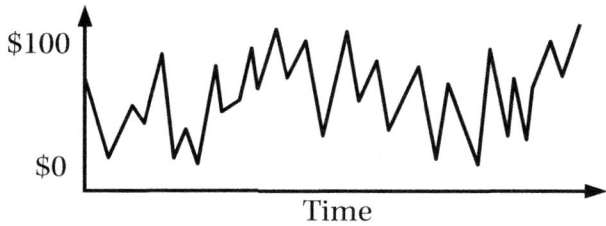

Suppose your goal is to train a model to predict unknown stock prices. The right approach is to hold out a test set, let's say 10% of the prices, to check if the model really predicts unseen prices. Machine learning software libraries come with built-in functionality to split data into training and test sets by randomly removing a percentage of the data points to create the test set.

Using the remaining portion of your dataset you then train your model to predict a price on a given date, based on features about prices around that date. For example, you use the average weekly price of a stock and its volatility around a date to predict the unknown price.

When you evaluate your model on the independent test set, it proves that the model predicts stock prices really well on unseen data. This attracts hordes of investors, who give you their millions to trade with, especially when you mention that you use AI. The folks of the Efficient Market Hypothesis were wrong after all.

But when you use your predictions to trade in real life, the result is a train wreck and you lose all your investors' money. What went wrong?

There were two problems with your approach. First, you used features like "average stock price *around* the date." Suppose you need to predict a stock price on a Wednesday. On the training data, you looked at the whole week, Monday to Friday, and computed the average stock price. But in real life, you can never know future prices. You can only compute the average price of Monday and Tuesday. This problem is known as a *look-ahead bias*. You should always make sure that a model is trained on features that can be calculated the same way in real life.

The second mistake was to select points randomly to create the test set. By doing this, some test points will fall before some training points. This means you're evaluating the capability of your model at predicting unseen prices from both past and future data. This is another instance of look-ahead bias, which made your first mistake go undetected.

In many cases, choosing random test data works well. For example, if you're classifying images into categories, you may select random images to evaluate your model, since there is no notion of past and future. But when the data is temporally correlated, as in stock prices, your test set should contain data that comes *after* the data in the training set.

It is common to make this kind of mistake, especially when copy-pasting somebody else's code or using off-the-shelf tools without giving them much thought. This is just another reminder that machine learning is not a one-size-fits-all solution; it's as important as ever to carefully take into account the characteristics of your problem.

In a company I used to work for, a data scientist developed a machine learning model to predict the likelihood that someone would buy a product for a certain price. It looked really promising. There was a slight look-ahead bias, but it was deemed that the risk of being fooled by it was low. Because of the positive results, he spent about two months refining the model, even hiring on-demand computer clusters at the price tag of a few thousand dollars.

At some point, just to check, he decided to make that extra effort to remove the slight look-ahead bias. The result was dreadful. It turns out the model hadn't learned anything meaningful. It had learned to cheat by exploiting that minor snooping into the future. To this day, we don't know exactly how it managed to do so. The lesson we did learn was to operate in the cleanest way possible, always.

Data leakage can happen in obscure ways. I once heard a story of a machine learning model that was suspiciously good at predicting whether or not a customer would buy a product. It was 100% accurate. Something was obviously wrong with it, but the model was quite complex and thus difficult to analyze. After investigating for a while, its creators discovered that the problem came from sloppy data preparation. When recording prices in the dataset, the price of a product that had been bought was recorded with one decimal digit after the dot, such as "$10.5." If the product hadn't been bought, its price was recorded with two digits, as in "$10.51." The model had learned to predict if a customer would buy a product based on the number of digits of precision of its price. The process was 100% accurate on past data, even when measured on the independent test set, but would never work in real life.

The take-home message here is, when doing machine learning, it is important to be diligent in the validation process and in the manipulation of the data.

MEASURING BUSINESS VALUE

You've spent all this time and money in developing a machine learning model that makes meaningful predictions, but was it worth it for your business? Will it impact your bottom line?

Assessing a model's performance at predicting things is not the same as assessing the business value that it brings. Improving the predictiveness of a model by 10% doesn't mean that it'll generate 10% more revenue for the business. It looks more like this:

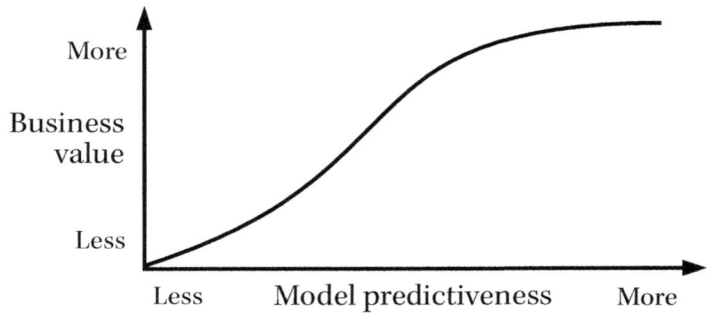

Increasing model predictiveness exhibits diminishing returns in terms of business value. Suppose that your machine learning model predicts the most relevant products for a user's search on your online store. Once you get to show the top five most relevant products in the results, you probably won't gain many more purchases by improving how these five results are sorted. And if you factor in the costs of improving the model, the curve could start bending downward at some point: improvements cost more than the value they bring.

It is thus important to measure the business value of machine learning. I've heard of companies who even degrade a model on purpose, smearing it a bit with questionable predictions. If they see that the downgraded model provides similar value as the best model, they infer that they've already reached the flat part of the curve above and there is no point in improving the model further.

A model's business value is measured on real customers. You need to expose different customers to different versions of the model and compare the outcomes, which is known as *A/B testing*. This is used beyond machine learning, for example, to assess the response of users to two alternative versions of an ad or two alternative designs of a website.

The first consideration you need to make is how to split customers into test groups for different models. One way to do it is at random, which is a good strategy from a statistical point of view. The caveat is that it could lead to a bad user experience. For example, the same user may see different results on repeated visits to your website, which could result in complaints. Suppose you are comparing two machine learning models used to sort products by relevance in an online store. Clients who see a different product at the top on repeated visits to your homepage are unlikely to get extremely angry. But if you're testing pricing models and the clients see different prices for the same product, you could soon be in the news. So, it's a business decision, not just a technical one, whether random A/B testing would be appropriate.

The alternative is to use some characteristic of the client or the request to decide which model to use. For example, you could choose the model based on the client's country. But you need to make sure that the criterion used doesn't leave you with groups that are too different from one another. For example, if you only expose customers from Switzerland to one model and from France to another one, your measurement is likely to be biased. This is because the two groups of customers have different purchasing power, which could explain a difference in the outcomes that has nothing to do with the model itself.

An approach that avoids this problem would split the incoming requests based on the parity of the client's IP address (even numbers go to model A, odd numbers go to model B). Unlike their country of residence, people's purchasing patterns don't depend on their IP addresses (which they probably don't even know). So this is an unbiased split. However, two people shopping in the same room could see a different product at the top of the results on their respective smartphones for the same search. As you can see, there are several ways to create test groups, each with its own caveats. And these were just a couple of examples. This decision could be the subject of long conversations between data scientists and the rest of the business. Once you've decided how to split the traffic, you have to try out the two models for some time and collect data on how they each perform. You need to track a value that is of interest to your business, one that matters for your business goals. This could be, for example, the revenue collected or the number of clicks.

If there is a difference in the measurement, you need to make sure that it is significant and not mere luck. This is done through statistical tests. If the model that performs best swaps on different days, there is too much natural variability in the figures to draw any conclusions. But if one method is better than the other consistently, for several days, it is likely that the difference is real and you'll have a good estimate of the incremental business value brought by the best of the models.

14

DEEP LEARNING

DEEP learning has become one of the trendiest buzzwords in the business world. Everyone wants to make everything deep. Just mention that you're doing deep learning and investors will flock to you.

But since I don't want you to be disappointed, I'll explain to you what deep learning is really about; if you thought it was just like any learning, but more profound, keep reading.

LEARNING FROM RAW DATA

Do you remember the model we created for Flixnet to predict customer behavior? The training dataset for that machine learning model contained descriptive features about the clients, including their age and the number of hours spent streaming video. Each of the features had a different meaning and was easy to interpret.

That is the kind of friendly input used by models in traditional machine learning. The task of the model is to map useful and interpretable features to a desired output prediction.

But what happens when your input does not come as a list of useful descriptors? Suppose the input is an image instead, and your task is to create a model that detects whether the image contains a cat. An image is just a matrix of numbers:

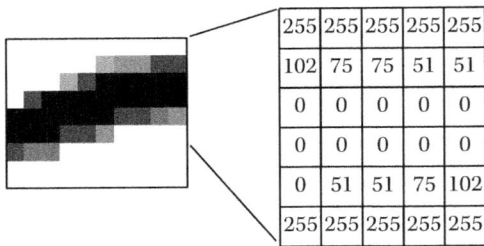

At every cell (or *pixel*), there is a number from 0 to 255 that indicates the intensity of light at that location. Suppose that the figure above is a portion of an image showing a cat's whisker against a white wall. The dark whisker is represented by the low numbers, close to zero, and the white background by the high numbers, close to 255.

But these numbers are not very helpful to describe the underlying subject. As humans, we recognize objects by shapes and patterns, not by numbers in a grid. A training dataset containing images is nothing like the Flixnet dataset. It doesn't contain meaningful features that the model could easily use to predict what's in the image.

In order to use traditional machine learning with images, you needed to first extract meaningful features to give the model something to work with. The whole thing was a two-step process:

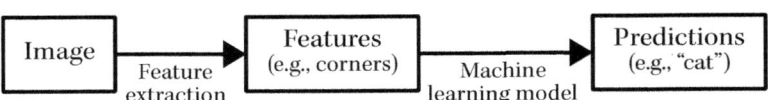

The first step involved running feature extraction algorithms on the raw input image (the matrix of numbers). These are algorithms especially designed to identify meaningful aspects of images, like corners and lines, by analyzing the pixel values. Usually, feature extraction has nothing to do with machine learning. It has to happen before the machine learning part of the process, and it uses handwritten algorithms based on human knowledge of how certain patterns appear in images and even gut feelings of what could be useful to extract from them.

After running this complicated feature extraction process, you would finally have a dataset much closer to that of Flixnet. For every image, you would have a list of representative features with some useful meaning. You could then move on to the second step of inputting these meaningful features to a machine learning model, as we've seen before. This long, complicated process is how things would run in a traditional machine learning model.

Deep learning is innovative because it learns directly from the raw data, like image pixel values, eliminating the need for the first step of feature extraction:

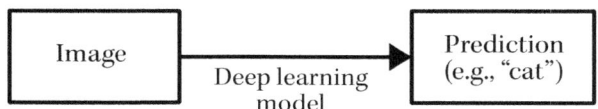

This is quite an ambitious task for the model to learn. It certainly needs to dig "deeper" because it is not given meaningful features on a silver platter. You'll soon see how this is achieved.

NEURAL NETWORKS

Do you remember that we used a straight-line model for Flixnet? In deep learning, the straight line is not the model of choice. A more powerful kind of model is used instead, known as an *artificial neural network* or just neural network. These have existed since the 1980s, so they are not an invention of deep learning. However, deep learning uses them in a different way. I will now show you how neural nets work in a traditional sense, and then we'll see how deep learning uses them in an innovative way to learn from complicated data.

Any machine learning model can be seen as a mathematical function. You take certain numbers (the inputs) and perform an operation to obtain another number (the prediction). For example, in Flixnet we had two inputs, the age of clients and for how long they streamed video last month. These numbers were combined to produce a prediction, which can also be seen as a number: an output of zero means that the client is deemed to leave, and a one means that the client is deemed to stay. The following is an example of a mathematical function that gives the same results as the straight-line model shown earlier in this book:

1.   Multiply the age by 3;

2.   Multiply the number of streaming hours by 4;

3.   Add those two results together;

4.   If the total is greater than 150, then output 1 (client stays); otherwise, output 0 (client leaves).

Believe it or not, this calculation conveys the exact same idea of checking on which side of the line a client falls in order to make a prediction. I carefully chose the numbers 3, 4 and 150 to define this process so that it matches the optimal straight-line model we saw earlier.

Similarly, determining whether a cat is in an image is a mathematical function. The input is a matrix of numbers (the image) and the output is either one or zero (there is or is not a cat). But this function is probably very complicated. Imagine how much you need to manipulate the pixel values of an image to transform them into a single one or zero that represents the presence or absence of a cat.

A neural network model seeks to represent really complicated functions. In order to do this, it breaks up a function into a network of very simple operations:

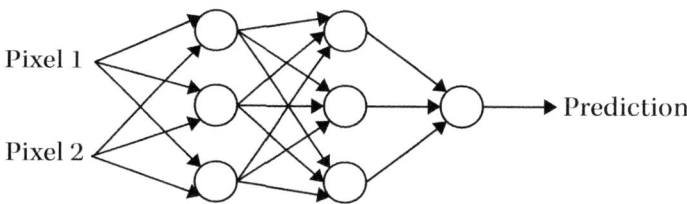

This illustration assumes that there are only two inputs (a simplistic image with just two pixels) and one output (the prediction of catness). Every circle represents a very simple mathematical operation that combines the numbers it receives, indicated by the arrows. The output of each operation is used as an input to the next operation until you reach the final prediction at the end. If you draw the journey of the initial numbers through the operations, you get a network like in the figure above, with several layers and connections. (This is a nice way to visualize it, but remember that for a programmer this is just another piece of code that performs all the calculations.)

Every circle is called a neuron. The operation performed by a neuron is, in general, a weighted sum of the inputs. This means that all the inputs are summed together but each of them is adjusted by a weight. For example, if a neuron has two inputs, its operation will look like this:

Weighted sum = input 1 * 2 + input 2 * 5

In this example, the value of one input is multiplied by the weight "2" and the other one by the weight "5" before adding them together. (We'll see how those weights are chosen in a bit.) Afterward, the weighted sum passes through a so-called *activation function*, used to squeeze it into a shorter range of numbers. A simple choice for this is a threshold function, as in the following example: if the weighted sum is greater than 20, output 1; otherwise, output 0.

And *voilà*, that's all neurons do. It's not very fancy, is it?

The exact calculation made by a neuron is wholly determined by the values of the weights (2 and 5 in the example above) and the threshold (20). Different values lead to different results. And the behavior of the entire network—that is, the function it computes—is determined by all the weights and thresholds across the different neurons. Note that a single neuron performs a calculation similar to the entire Flixnet model, as we discussed a minute ago.

So, where does machine learning fit into all this? It has been proven that if a network has enough neurons it can be configured to compute *any* function (or an approximation of it). For example, if there is a function that takes an image and determines if there is a cat in it, then there also exists a neural network to compute it. So, neural networks are a very powerful kind of model—much more so than the straight-line model we saw before.

But there's a catch. You need to know the right combination of weights and thresholds so that the network does what you want. These values are the moving parts of the model, the parameters (like the coordinates of the straight line we met before) which are learned from data.

To set up a neural network, a data scientist first chooses the network architecture: the number of layers, neurons and connections. These are all fixed and decided beforehand. Then the right values of the parameters are learned from a training dataset using a gradient descent optimization algorithm.

The optimization starts from a network with random parameters. That means that the network is initially configured to compute a nonsensical function that almost certainly doesn't do what you want. The optimizer then uses the training data, such as images with their corresponding true labels, to quantify the network's error at performing the task (the cost function, remember?). It then slightly tweaks the parameters of the network so that it becomes better at the task (and the cost is reduced). The process is repeated over and over again, progressively improving the function represented by the network.

Suppose the optimization succeeded in finding a combination of parameters (weights and thresholds) that gives predictions with low error. This means the network is now configured to compute a useful function that does what you want. But how exactly is the network doing that? No one knows.

In such an entangled network of products, sums and thresholds, you will have a hard time understanding how a network comes up with a good prediction. You simply have to trust the result. You may want to have a look at some of the learned weights, but when there are thousands of them, you'll soon get lost. That's why the neurons in the inner layers of a network are said to be *hidden*. You'll probably never understand what a network does inside. The data scientist only provides the end goal to the optimization algorithm, and the network configures itself internally to perform the given task.

This all looks like magic, right? Neural networks learn really complicated functions without you doing much more than deciding how many neurons to put in the network. Amazing! But wait—not so fast!

RESTRICTED NEURAL NETWORKS

In theory, a neural network may be configured to compute any function. But no one said that finding the right combination of weights and thresholds to achieve that would be easy. It's like looking for a needle in a haystack. The optimization algorithm is prone to getting stuck and thus giving poor solutions, and the more parameters it has to learn, the worse these problems get.

If you look at the previous figure of a neural net, you'll see that I connected every neuron with *all* the neurons in the previous layer. That has been the common way to do it since the '80s. This was to satisfy the ambition of using neural networks to compute complex functions: the more connections, the more complex a function a network can learn.

But suppose you connect every pixel of an image of size 1000 × 1000 with 100 hidden neurons:

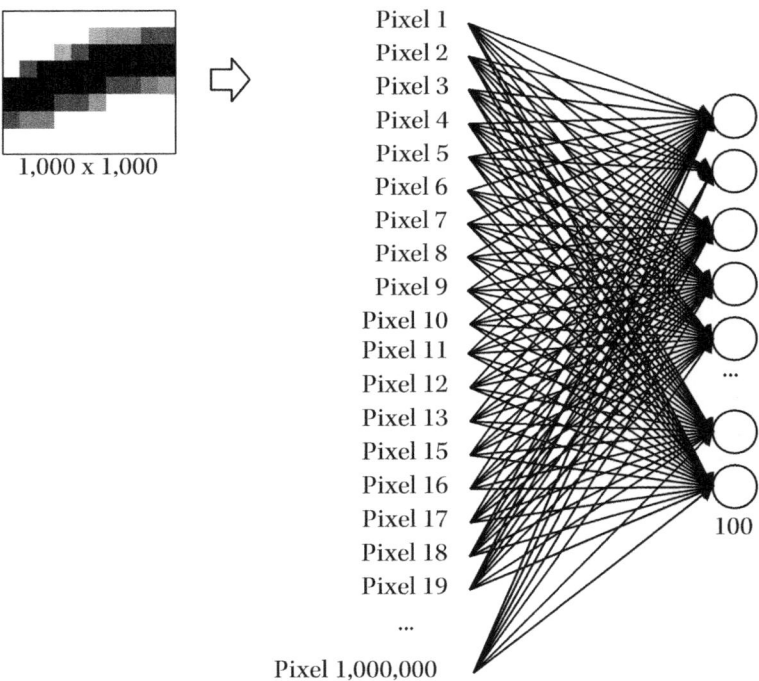

This network looks really entangled. It has 100 million connections. Remember that each connection here represents taking the pixel value and multiplying it by a learnable weight. All the weighted values are then summed inside the neuron and passed through a threshold.

If we count all the weights and thresholds, this network has 100,000,100 parameters whose ideal values the optimization algorithm needs to find. And remember that it starts from completely random ones. Given the sheer number of parameters, it is very unlikely that your model will ever hit a good combination of values. And this is just for a single layer of neurons. Now imagine how big your haystack would become if you stacked twenty layers like this one, instead of using just one.

This brings us to another innovation brought in by deep learning: *restricted neural networks.* This approach made it possible to train large neural networks. The secret is to severely *restrict* the connections, either by outright eliminating connections (sometimes thousands of them) or forcing many of the weights to take the same values instead of moving independently, to dramatically reduce the number of parameters. With fewer moving parts, your haystack just got much smaller.

It may seem counterintuitive that limiting what the network can learn improves the results, but it does so because a good solution is easier to find when you have fewer places to look. But you also wouldn't want to wipe out good solutions by adding restrictions. That's why the restrictions need to be carefully designed: they have to make sense with your problem and your kind of input so that the best solution still exists among the remaining candidates.

Let's look now at a type of restricted layer commonly used in object recognition, known as *convolutional*. In this type of layer, every neuron is connected only to a small spatial neighborhood of values from the previous layer, as opposed to the entire thing:

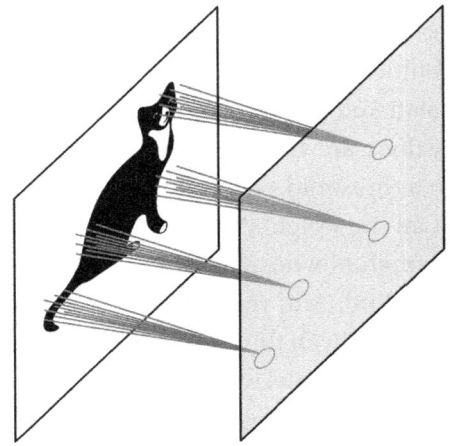

This illustration shows four example neurons, but there are usually a lot more, spanning the entire image. Each neuron, however, only "sees" a little portion of the image.

This sort of restriction is based on the principle that an object can be detected by its parts. Basic visual patterns, such as edges and lines, and even more sophisticated ones, like eyes or whiskers, rarely span an entire image, and it is thus okay to only look at a few neighboring spaces at once. Another useful principle is that the logic needed to find objects is often the same in every part of the image. For example, an eye at the top left of the image can be detected the same way as an eye in the bottom right. This principle is also exploited by convolutional layers to bring down the number of learnable parameters even further. These simplifications significantly reduce the number of connections without wiping out good solutions.

If I rewrote the entangled layer I showed you above as a convolutional layer, I'd go from over a hundred million learnable values to less than two thousand. Now things are starting to look more manageable.

Convolutional neural networks, or CNNs, have become one of the most popular types of models in the image analysis field.

THE DEEP LEARNING'S EDGE

With deep learning methods, we can now use neural networks to learn directly from complicated data, like images and audio. The most obvious advantage is that it simplifies the old two-step process, which required slow and cumbersome feature extraction algorithms.

But that's not all there is. It turns out that deep neural networks also exhibit a higher predictive performance than the previous two-step approaches. For example, deep learning for speech recognition, trained directly on raw audio recordings, makes better predictions than the older two-step methods, trumping decades of research on algorithms to extract meaningful features from audio. The reason for this is that the network learns, in a data-driven way, how to extract useful information from the input to solve the problem, instead of trusting a limited set of features that a data scientist decided were important.

Another less obvious advantage of using just a neural network, without the previous feature extraction process, is that it can be run really fast. Since all this involves is a regular sequence of simple operations, such as sums and products, the execution can be significantly accelerated on a graphics card, even inside a mobile device. Before, the algorithms to extract meaningful features had to be run separately and often ended up being quite time-consuming.

ARCHITECTS OF SENSIBLE RESTRICTIONS

With less effort and better results, deep learning may seem like an amazing silver bullet. But building a deep neural network is not effortless or "hands-off." You need to design the appropriate architecture for your problem, the number and types of layers. In fact, some of the effort spent in the feature extraction of the old two-step process has now shifted toward network design. But it tends to pay off well.

The essential task for a data scientist doing deep learning is to find clever ways of introducing restrictions. I like to call these *sensible restrictions*. For example, convolutional layers, which only focus on a small neighborhood of pixels at a time, are sensible for object recognition. However, that may not be the sensible thing to do in another field. For example, if you want to outline the boundaries of an object, rather than just detecting it, then convolutional networks are not as good.

Deep learning has found its success in a number of popular applications, such as the analysis of images, video, speech and text, because researchers have found great restricted architectures for them. But what if your problem is completely different? For example, suppose you're working on facial recognition, but instead of a picture of a person, your input is a 3-D representation of a face made up of a list of polygons described by the vertices' coordinates. In this case, it is not straightforward to use deep neural networks.

Deep learning is probably a good candidate when the input is a repetitive sequence of similar things that individually mean very little. For example, the pixels of an image, frames of a video, or words of a sentence. But if your data comes as a set of meaningful features, such as a list of clients with their ages, countries and purchases, deep learning is likely not the answer. In those cases, you're better off using other types of models, such as the popular gradient-boosted trees, or even the simple straight line we discussed earlier.

In the midst of all the hype, it is worth recalling that deep learning is not a magic wand: it exploits a set of human-designed restrictions that make particular sense to solve one problem and may not necessarily apply to *any* problem.

15

BEYOND SUPERVISED LEARNING

In 2015, a computer beat a human professional for the first time at the game Go. This sounds like no big deal, considering the highly publicized defeat of the chess world champion by IBM in 1985. But Go is different: the number of possible games is trillions of trillions of trillions of times larger than chess. The innovative Go algorithm used machine learning to solve this difficult problem.

So far, we've discussed cases in which machine learning models are trained from labeled data. For example, each image is accompanied by its true category, such as "animal" or "airplane." The model is designed to predict the category based on the input. This is known as *supervised* learning.

But not every machine learning problem can be formulated this way. There are certain problems where there is no clear-cut "true" label. Playing Go is one of them.

While supervised learning is very common, you are likely to encounter problems that need to be solved by other paradigms.

This chapter goes over some of these alternative formulations. It will give you a more complete picture of what machine learning can do.

UNSUPERVISED LEARNING

There is a type of machine learning known as *unsupervised*, which doesn't take labeled samples. I'm not a big fan of this name because it makes it sound magical, as if it learned from thin air. Despite its name, unsupervised learning is not simply a more advanced version of supervised learning. In reality, it is used to solve completely different problems than those of supervised learning, and some human input is always needed to tune the model.

The most common application of unsupervised learning is to find commonalities among different data points. For example, suppose you want to group all your customers into five categories, but you don't know exactly what these categories should be.

You can do this by unsupervised learning, using a so-called clustering algorithm to automatically split the clients into five groups, so that customers are very similar to each other inside each group but different across groups. But you need to define by hand what makes two customers similar. Is age an important factor? What is the relative importance between age and location to determine similarity? You can only use the clustering algorithm once you've figured that out.

Unsupervised learning is also used to detect anomalies. For example, you create a model of the most common purchase patterns from past customer data. If a new customer differs significantly from the model, it is deemed anomalous. This could be used, for example, to detect fraudulent user accounts.

This is a useful type of machine learning, mostly used to find common patterns in data. But it can't be used for anything.

For example, you can't use unsupervised learning to magically classify images of animals into "cat" and "dog" without any human-made labels.

TRIAL AND ERROR

Online advertisers are constantly choosing which ad to show you from a number of available ads. They want to select the *best* ad for you, the one you're most likely to click on based on your interests.

Machine learning is often used for this. You may collect past experience of who clicked on which ad. But this dataset does not contain the "true" labels of which ad is best for each client. The best ad could be one that wasn't shown at all to the client. You can't know unless you try. Therefore, traditional supervised learning is hard to use in this context because you can't just give the model a set of true labels to learn from.

The pricing of products works in a similar way. If you charge $20 for a T-shirt, you can't know if that's the best price, the one that maximizes revenue, unless you try other prices. Suppose you change the price to $30. You can now measure if the extra ten dollars you're charging compensates for the decrease in demand due to the higher price. But you need to try—just seeing that a T-shirt was sold for $20 in the past doesn't give you the "true" label of how much you should have charged for it.

In these contexts, machine learning models are trained by trial and error. Different alternatives are dynamically tried to measure the user's reaction and collect feedback. For example, when advertisers don't know anything about you, they show you random ads. As you click on some of the ads, they start to build a profile about your interests and start to show you ads that are especially targeted to you.

However, learning by trial and error has its costs. You have to choose how often you give a chance to solutions different from the one you believe so far to be the best. For example, if your model predicts that the client is interested in buying a vacuum cleaner, how often should you show completely unrelated ads, say for travel, just to learn more about the client?

Choosing alternative options is known as *exploration*. The more you do it the more information you gather and the more confident you can be about your predictions. For example, if you were wrong about the vacuum cleaner in the first place, you will catch it soon enough if you explore alternatives. You could stumble upon another product that the client is more drawn to than a vacuum.

But exploring has an opportunity cost to it. If you were right about the vacuum cleaner, but keep showing unrelated ads to explore other options, you keep missing opportunities to show the relevant ad. At some point, you want to trust the knowledge you have and show vacuum ads most of the time, which is known as *exploitation* because you exploit the knowledge you've mustered.

One of the great challenges of learning by trial and error is to balance the trade-off between exploration and exploitation. There are different strategies to do that. The simplest one is to always explore a fixed percentage of time. For example, 10% of the time is dedicated to exploring an alternative instead of using the alleged best option. Another way to do this is to use a more sophisticated algorithm, which progressively lowers the amount of exploration of alternatives that don't prove fruitful.

The context also changes with time. For example, the client may end up buying a vacuum cleaner and thus not be interested in acquiring a second one. Therefore, you can't just stop exploring altogether once you've found the customer's interests. This is one of the many considerations you have to make when designing a trial-and-error learning algorithm.

Trial-and-error algorithms are known as *multi-armed ban-*

dits. This is a sort of joke: a "one-armed bandit" is slang for a slot machine. But here you have multiple arms to choose from, such as the ads to show or products to recommend.

REINFORCEMENT LEARNING

When choosing which ad to display to a user, you obtain feedback on your action right away. The user either clicks on the ad or doesn't. The reward, or lack thereof, is observed immediately.

But, in some problems, you're interested in maximizing the long-term reward of your actions, not just the immediate reward. Such is the case of games, for example. Making any single move often doesn't exhibit any direct reward, but it impacts your overall chances of winning the game later on.

Or suppose you want an autonomous car to learn by itself how to parallel park. You let the car try many actions, but it only gets the reward when it fits into the parking space. But parking successfully may require the car to take actions that bring it away from its goal, like pulling ahead of the space before reversing back into it. So your self-driving car model can't just "think" one step ahead.

Reinforcement learning is the branch of machine learning that studies these kinds of problems. The goal is to learn a *policy*, a strategy to choose actions that maximizes the long-term payoff.

There are many ways to tackle a reinforcement learning problem, and there is much research dedicated to the topic. One way is to train a model to estimate the *value* of taking an action, how positive the effect of that action would be in the long run.

This is similar to what goes on in your mind when you're playing a game. You constantly estimate how much value it would bring you to make each of the possible moves. You then make the move that you think provides the highest value. If you're a good player it means you're good at making value estimations.

Suppose this is the current state of a tic-tac-toe game:

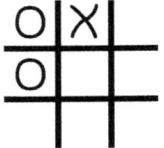

You're next and have to place a cross. You estimate that put-ting a cross in the middle cell offers a value of zero, or even neg-ative, because it would let your opponent win in the next round (you're thinking two steps ahead). Therefore, you decide not to put a cross there and choose a different move.

Similarly, in reinforcement learning, a machine learning model is trained to estimate the value of making a move given the current state of the game:

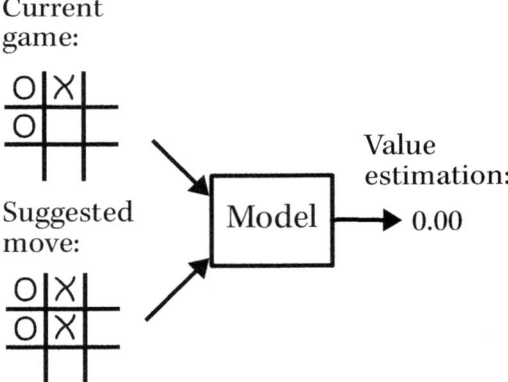

The model estimating the value of each move inside its black box is what defines the playing strategy. When this model is used in real life to beat a human player, the program looks at the value predicted for all possible moves and picks the one that would provide the highest value. Similarly, the model to park a car would provide a value estimation for each possible action (reverse, turn left, and so on) and it would perform the most valuable one.

The model used in AlphaGo, the famous Go algorithm, is a deep convolutional neural network. If you remember from the previous chapter, convolutional networks are used to detect objects in images. They are built upon a number of intuitive principles, such as only looking at a few neighboring pixels at a time. This translates very well to Go. Since this game is played on a board with a grid layout, each cell is analogous to the pixel of an image. Instead of analyzing a group of pixels at a time, AlphaGo analyzes a group of nearby game cells at a time.

In object recognition, the images in the training data set are labeled with their correct categories: "plane," "strawberry," etc. But how do you train a model in reinforcement learning when you don't know in advance the true value of every possible action?

It goes something like this. Suppose your goal is to train a game-playing model. You start from an initial random model, which means that the playing strategy is completely bogus. You then use that "strategy" to simulate a game between two players, all the way to the end. At each step, a player typically chooses the best move according to the model (exploitation), which generates realistic games. Sometimes, though, the players choose an alternative move at random (exploration), which gives variability to the simulation.

The game finishes at some point, when one of the players wins. Now you can generate training labels, as follows: You select some or all of the moves in the game made by the winner and give them label 1 (good move). You then select moves by the loser and give them label -1 (bad move).

These labels can now be used to improve the model, as in a traditional classification problem. Your model's goal is to classify moves as good or bad. The parameters of the model (for example, the weights of a neural network) are updated so that the model outputs a higher value for good moves and a lower value for bad moves. This is a single baby step of an optimization by gradient descent, which tries to make the model slightly better at performing the task. Now the game-playing strategy is better than before.

You may have noticed that the 1 and -1 labels are really noisy. The fact that the winner made a certain move doesn't make that move necessarily good. But you hope that this process, if repeated several times, will give more 1s than -1s to good moves.

Once you've finished the first update, you need to simulate a new game. You can start this new game from scratch or choose an intermediate game at random from the previous simulation. The game is played again all the way to the end, now using the improved model as a guiding strategy. You then create the 1 and -1 labels and use them to update the model again.

After repeating this process tens of millions of times, the model may learn a good strategy to play the game.

The first version of AlphaGo used both supervised and reinforcement learning. The supervised part learned from a dataset of moves labeled "good" or "bad," created by recording thousands of human plays. Afterward, reinforcement learning was used to improve that model. A new version of AlphaGo was released two years later, known as AlphaGo Zero, which started from a random model and learned only from self-playing, through a process similar to the one I've just shown you.

THE BOTTOM LINE

In the traditional supervised approach, a model learns from data that contains the true label for every sample. Since labeled data is inconvenient to gather, it is tempting to look at alternative approaches.

But the choice to use an alternative approach, such as trial and error, often isn't yours to make. It depends on the problem. For example, how would you train a translation system by trial and error? You would need to collect feedback on which translations are good or bad. Data scientists are certainly trying to do it. Facebook, for example, will ask you to rate a translation. But the amount of feedback collected is extremely scarce. Furthermore, you would also need to do exploration, where you'd produce randomly altered translations just to learn from the feedback. Imagine the poor user experience you would give people by intentionally producing translations with words that didn't make sense, just to collect data on them. For advertisements, it is different: no one's going to be seriously offended by being shown an irrelevant ad.

Reinforcement learning, a more sophisticated form of the trial-and-error approach, has received the most attention in recent times. But there are two caveats. First, a model needs a lot of experience to learn from. For example, it took three days of self-playing for AlphaGo Zero to beat the original AlphaGo algorithm and over 40 days of self-playing to outperform all other approaches. Even a simple console game requires the equivalent to over 80 hours of human playing to learn how to play competitively. This probably explains why most applications of reinforcement learning involve learning from a simulated environment. For example, a game can be simulated millions of times algorithmically, and you'd always know the winner. Or you can simulate in a computer the movements of a car trying to parallel park— instead of having an actual car do it—and you would know how well it eventually parked in the space. But this isn't always the case. For example, with translations or adverts, you need human feedback to tell you if something worked or not, which is much slower and more costly to obtain.

The second caveat is that training a reinforcement learning

algorithm is tricky. Slight changes in the way you train it can lead to significantly different results. This makes a successful method hard to reproduce in practice. Designing how you measure the value of a move is also a difficult task. For example, you may want to encourage your system to win the game as early as possible instead of just winning at some point. Or you may want a vehicle to learn how to park fast, not just park someday. All of this needs to be carefully tuned, and doing so is not straightforward.

AlphaGo had a significant advantage that made it a winning model. The game of Go has a convenient structure: a board with a grid layout. This allowed AlphaGo's developers to import the well-known convolutional neural networks used in image analysis. In fact, I find it quite funny that every AI algorithm that makes the headlines seems to use a convolutional net. But what about all the problems in life that can't be formulated as a grid of numbers?

The simpler one-step trial-and-error approach, the multi-armed bandit, is popular in advertising, recommendation and personalization. But its sophisticated cousin, reinforcement learning, hasn't yet found much success in the business world. We'll see in the future if it's possible to overcome its limitations.

16

THE LIMITS OF MACHINE LEARNING

Robots will soon replace all human labor, right? In a couple of years, all cars will drive themselves and your shopping will be delivered by a self-flying drone. Not so fast! Machine learning has its own set of limitations. Let's have a look.

Computers don't beat humans as often as you might think.

The promoters of AI often claim that machine learning "beats humans." I suggest you to be wary of such claims. For starters, how is human performance measured exactly? I've seen researchers measure how often two humans disagree when labeling images and use the resulting figure as the measure of human error. I've also seen researchers borrow the human error figure from someone else's research, conducted on a different problem and with different data. Those are not the best ways to do it.

The most accurate way to measure human error is to compare human performance against the truth, if there's a way to obtain that. For example, you may compare the result of a biopsy with a doctor's diagnosis. But this is not always easy to do.

But even then, measuring human error is, so to speak, error prone. First of all, which humans do you choose? Suppose your AI algorithm classifies images of birds into their species. Should you measure human error by asking your next-door neighbor to perform the task, or should you ask an ornithologist (a person who studies birds)? I personally can't tell the difference between a duck, a goose and a turkey, so my error rate would be pretty high.

Second, humans get tired. Even the most careful ornithologist would get bored when asked to label 10,000 images of birds by hand. In fact, that's a great way to promote machine learning: a computer doesn't get tired and its work quality is consistent. But neither of those qualities gives it a superior level of "intelligence."

There also tends to be a bias in the AI results you hear about. Scientific journals often only publish methods that beat competitors. Therefore, researchers are encouraged to share the things that worked and conceal the ones that didn't. Everything in the literature ends up having a positive spin. This is also true in the business world, where companies oversell to investors the capabilities of machine learning. Even data scientists oversell their results to their own managers. This creates a snowball effect of exaggerated claims about the power of machine learning. So then, when you try to implement something in your own company, you end up disappointed when you realize how rule-bound computers really are.

A few years ago, I attended a conference where one of the speakers claimed that her machine learning model beat humans at the task of classifying sketches into categories, such as "guitar" or "panda." She also showed examples of failures, but these were very close calls and on sketches that weren't very skillfully drawn. For example, the algorithm confused a guitar with a violin, but the input drawing was too simplistic for anyone to tell the difference. Another example was a drawing of a windmill, which the algorithm misclassified as a fan.

The impression one got was that the speaker was showing failures that weren't real failures only to highlight even more how accurate her method was. It was like when job seekers are asked for their weaknesses and they answer, "I am too hard-working."

A member of the public (I swear it wasn't me) asked her if she could show examples of *real* failures instead. Unsurprisingly, the speaker had not prepared any other failure cases to show that day.

COMPUTERS MAKE MISTAKES A HUMAN NEVER WOULD.

Even if an algorithm is 99.5% accurate, you should analyze what's in that remaining 0.05% of failure. Are those errors all close calls, such as confusing a violin with a guitar? The reality of current machine learning models is that errors can be quite extreme. There is a funny example in which a machine learning model, when given a picture of a baby holding a toothbrush, labeled the image as "a young boy holding a baseball bat." Confusing a toothbrush with a baseball bat is a mistake a human would never make. That algorithm performed pretty well when evaluated *numerically* by using typical error metrics; however, if you only quantify errors by counting them, you fall into the trap of ignoring the fact that some of them are *qualitatively* worse than others. That is to say, this model didn't make many mistakes, but some of the mistakes it did make were very, very wrong.

With that in mind, would you let an AI algorithm fly your

airplane or drive your car? A few years ago, there was a massive hype around self-driving cars. I was apprehensive of that field: considering that state-of-the-art algorithms make mistakes that a human would never make, I didn't see self-driving cars roaming the street anytime soon. Also, most prototypes use deep neural networks. If you remember, it is really hard to know how a neural network comes up with a prediction. Therefore, from a legal standpoint, I didn't see those vehicles being approved when they were built around algorithms that couldn't be understood.

It may seem that we're almost there because computers already fly planes and drive trains. But autopilots operate in a predictable environment and don't use machine learning. On the other hand, self-driving cars have to react to jaywalkers or decide between hitting a pedestrian or crashing against another vehicle. Unsurprisingly, year after year, companies have been saying that they need just one more year to launch their self-driving vehicles.

In fact, the more dangerous or life-critical a system the less likely people are to adopt machine learning for it. A few years ago, I spent a day at the defense department of a government, hearing out their needs and advising them on machine learning. They were particularly interested in using AI to identify objects in satellite images. Throughout our conversations, they insisted on the fact that the system shouldn't miss a target, ever; otherwise, they would still manually inspect every corner of the image, which would negate the use of an automated system in the first place. In their field, mistakes can cost people's lives. The operators are also held personally responsible for what they find (or miss) in the images. A mistake can easily cost a career. Their threshold for accepting any AI solution was 100% accuracy. Considering that the most sophisticated techniques still confuse a toothbrush with a baseball bat, I don't think that's going to happen.

YOU NEED DATA.

Machine learning is hungry for data and often lots of it. In many cases, such as the images used to train object recognition models, the data has to be annotated by hand. The numbers are staggering: there are datasets of over 10 million images, annotated by humans one by one. A friend of mine from grad school and his colleague once had to manually inspect and annotate 200,000 images to train a model. I heard it wasn't fun.

Some businesspeople overlook the data aspect of training a model. They just want to do things with AI, ignoring that it needs something to learn from. This reminds me of an incident from a few years ago. After a knife attack at a train station in France, a politician suggested that AI would soon predict those dangerous events from CCTV footage. But how is that going to work exactly? You would need a database with tens of thousands of images of stabbings in public places. I sincerely hope we don't have data from that many incidents. I don't blame this politician for his comment though: with the constant praise for machine learning, people end up thinking it can do anything in the blink of an eye.

Another data-hungry application is automatic translation. These systems are trained on documents that have been translated by humans before, pairs of the same document in different languages side by side. The model is supposed to learn how to transform a document on one side into the one on the other side. For example, the first Google Translate was trained on thousands of documents from the UN and the European Parliament because they are routinely translated by humans into different languages.

Even if you created a perfect machine translation system, what is going to happen when new words appear in a language?

The current systems rely on the translations made by humans before, so you would need a constant inflow of new human-translated data to adapt to changes in the language. It might be tempting to think that an intelligent system could automatically infer the meaning of the word from the context or something like that. There is, in fact, ongoing research in that direction. But this is nowhere near the reality of how current machine learning works.

Maintaining a good dataset can be challenging even if you're not doing fancy object recognition or machine translation. For example, suppose you want to predict whether a customer will click on a product from your online store. All you need to do is to collect past data of which clients clicked and which didn't. You don't have to annotate this data, just collect it. But this requires clients, who are human beings, to perform this behavior in the first place. It will take a while to gather a substantial amount of data from clients, especially if your business is small. The conditions of the market also change with time, which means you have to keep gathering data and retraining your models periodically.

SOME DETAILS OF THE MODEL ARE ALWAYS DECIDED IN ADVANCE.

All machine learning models have a fixed structure in them, which is not learned from data. The learning process only adjusts the portions of the model that haven't been fixed. The fixed structure must be decided by its creator in a problem-specific way. For example, when data scientists train a neural network, they predefine the number of neurons, layers and connections. The learning process only adjusts the values that configure the operation inside each neuron; it does not add or remove neurons. We also saw a straight-line model, which learned the position of the line but wasn't allowed to do anything else with it, like bending it into a curve.

It is tempting to "liberate" the fixed parts of a model, thinking this would improve the results by letting the model learn anything it wants. However, this doesn't work in practice. A very flexible model is hard to train because, given all the choice, we're back to looking for a needle in a haystack. A model with no fixed structure will also be prone to learning bogus patterns that don't have any real meaning.

The most successful models have a fixed structure that is especially relevant to the characteristics of the problem. For example, the convolutional neural networks used in object recognition are especially designed to take into account principles of object recognition. In fact, often a smaller network that is more adapted to a problem can outperform a larger, generic network. I once created a neural network that was 100 times *smaller* than a competitor model, but it produced better (and faster) predictions. This happened because I designed it more carefully, taking the characteristics of the problem into account instead of just going big.

Behind every model there is always a human making at least a few design decisions. As certain practices become common, they are packaged into off-the-shelf solutions. For example, there are "automatic machine learning" tools, which try out many different types of models and choose the best one. These tools systematize tasks that a data scientist would have performed manually. But this doesn't effectively remove the need for human supervision for two reasons. First, any greenfield problem is unlikely to be solved by an off-the-shelf solution. Second, the less thought you give to your solution the more you can end up with a model that works well just by chance but won't make good predictions in real life.

THERE IS NO UNIVERSALLY BEST TYPE OF MODEL.

As in other fields, there is a "no free lunch" principle in machine learning, formalized by David Wolpert in 1996. It states that there is no universal best type of machine learning model. Some are indeed superior to others in certain contexts, but this is because they make appropriate assumptions about the context.

But assumptions are not universal and may not stand in a different problem. For example, deep learning for image recognition is built upon assumptions about the field, such as the fact that an object can be detected by the presence of its parts. This assumption may not be true, or useful, for solving other problems.

Another way to see the "no free lunch" principle is that there are no problem-independent reasons to favor one type of model over another. It is only when you consider the details of a problem that you can decide which model to use.

You may encounter some people who seem to have an infatuation with a certain type of model, trying to use it at all cost. They want to make everything *deep*. But the best approach is to analyze the problem to see what kind of model serves it best.

HIGH PERFORMANCE MAY SACRIFICE EXPLAINABILITY.

The more complex a model the less you can understand how it comes up with its predictions. For example, the deep neural networks used in image recognition exhibit the highest performance in the field, but little is known about how they work internally. This is great if what you're after is the highest predictive performance. However, sometimes business requires explainability.

I once developed a model for an online travel agency that

predicted the most appealing flight for a customer to be shown at the top of the search results. I could have done this with a sophisticated algorithm, with a high predictive power that would detect serendipitous patterns in past customer purchase behavior. However, the business wanted to indicate *why* the flight was the best one, such as "shortest layover." The best solution was to create a simpler model that could be thoroughly understood.

Striking the right balance between predictability and explainability is often an important part of the job, to the great disappointment of the nerdiest of machine learning practitioners.

A MODEL MAY NOT GENERALIZE WELL.

You can borrow somebody else's machine learning model and use it to address your own problem. This spares you the time and effort required to create everything from scratch. However, you may be disappointed with the result. If your problem is different from the original one, the predictions can be really poor. While models are intended to generalize to unseen data, this doesn't work with *any* data.

Suppose someone trained a model to count the number of pedestrians from a street camera. You want to use the same model to count the number of passengers on a train platform. The camera is different, the lighting is different and the movement patterns of people are different. There is no guarantee that this will work at all. I once took a deep neural network trained to detect buildings in aerial images taken over the United States and used it on an image of Zürich, captured with a different device. The network classified the entire Lake Zürich as a large building.

Models can often be shared and reused. After all, why reinvent the wheel? Sometimes, a borrowed model works right away. Other times, you need some effort to adapt it to your problem. In other cases, you're better off starting from square one.

Humans and computers are each good at different tasks.

A while ago, one of my relatives shared on Facebook a film poster with the following comment: "I loved her." It had been automatically translated by Facebook from its original language. The correct translation should have been "I loved it" (the movie). In English, inanimate objects are not referred to as "he" or "she" (with some metaphoric exceptions). But in Spanish, the original language of the post, all objects have genders, and a movie is female. The automatic translation turned the female word into "her."

The translation algorithm probably made the most correct decision: if, in the training dataset, the most common translation of similar phrases was to use "her" instead of "it," then it was the most sensible choice. I am sorry if this disappoints you, but automatic translation systems do not *understand* the message. Instead, they translate based on the most common way in which something was translated in the past. It is a game of probabilities.

There is a special kind of machine learning practitioner: staunch fans, who religiously defend AI at all costs. They have an answer for everything. They would argue that my previous example was unfair because the translation system didn't analyze the film poster. They would suggest creating an image-understanding algorithm to parse the images that come with a post, to aid the translation. In this case, the improved system would understand that the post is speaking about a movie and would translate the phrase accordingly.

This sounds like a solution, but there are many cases in which automatic translations go wrong. You could potentially create a new machine learning model to address each type of failure. But this line of thinking is really impractical. You need a dedicated, sophisticated solution to overcome each of the minor exceptions in the original system. This can go on forever. The payoff of spending time and resources to improve the system would exhibit diminishing returns. And every additional model suffers from all the problems described in this chapter, such as gathering data and choosing the model structure. Even the hunger for processing power to train the models could become prohibitive.

What religious AI fans overlook is that humans and computers are each good at different, complementary things. Computers are great at prescriptive, algorithmic tasks, which they solve at lightning-fast speed. In fact, I can assure you that my calculator beats both of us at performing multiplications.

At the same time, machines struggle at tasks that are exceedingly easy for humans, such as recognizing objects in an image. Even babies or dogs can beat AI in some problems. Strategic tasks, which require a solid body of knowledge and social awareness, are the hardest for a computer.

I had several conversations with an entrepreneur who wanted to use AI to automatically make strategic decisions for corporations, such as whether to open a new branch or cancel the development of a product. I didn't see that happening, though, because it is a complex and ill-posed problem, which is where humans excel and computers do not. How would you get the data to train a model to make good strategic decisions? The most important decisions in an organization are made in times of adversity, such as a global pandemic or a financial crash, for which you don't have many past training samples to learn from. Would you trust a model of the past to automatically decide whether to close a branch in an unprecedented context? Would you trust a model that makes silly mistakes to translate your legal documents?

Hardcore machine learning fanatics almost religiously claim that we're close to creating artificial human brains. In fact, the authors of some well-known scientific articles in the deep learning field justify their choices by drawing parallels to neuroscience. The truth, though, is that we don't know some of the most basic things about how a human brain works, but we can explain how an artificial neural network works in a few pages. I have heard researchers in AI confidently assert that human brains are just like large Turing machines. Without getting too philosophical, let me remark that this implies that we do not have free will: every single action that we take is the result of a programmed instruction in our brains.

When it comes to doing business, it is best to see machine learning as an improved way of defining algorithms. In the past, we would write an entire algorithm by hand, end to end. With machine learning, we fix some aspects of the solution and automatically learn the rest in a data-driven way. No wonder machine learning, in other languages, is known as "automatic learning."

Instead of saying that machines have become better than humans at detecting objects, it is more accurate to say that machines are better than humans at *defining the process* of detecting objects. In fact, it is not surprising that they're better at it, for the same reason calculators beat humans at doing multiplications: computers beat humans in the tedious task of defining all the specific steps required to detect an object in an image. Human brains, on the other hand, excel at just looking at an image and ignoring the irrelevant parts to pick out the object, without even realizing the process behind such a seemingly simple task.

You hopefully now understand how machine learning works, what it really involves to design and train a model. It's a powerful approach, but we've also been through its limitations. As you can see, machine learning is just another tool in the toolbox. And, like a hammer or a wrench, it doesn't suit every problem. Given all the challenges mentioned in this chapter, I can assure you that the world will not be taken over by robots any time soon.

17

THE FIVE COMMANDMENTS OF AI

So many things are being said about AI. You may be wondering whether your business should invest in AI too, if you haven't already done so. Or you might be wondering what you would and what you wouldn't use AI for. Let me share some personal advice on this. Here we go.

I.   YOU DON'T HAVE TO USE AI.

Just because everyone else is doing it doesn't mean it will work for you. You have to see if you have a business need that can be met with AI.

Some companies want to do AI just because they have data, even though they don't know exactly what to do with it. But AI is no different from anything else in the business world: first comes the problem, then the solution. Otherwise, you're doing things backwards. I've seen companies recruit data scientists just to see if they can find a way of extracting value from data. A business may choose to invest in cutting-edge innovation with unpredictable results. But they should remember that it may not turn out the way they want.

What you *do* have to do is collect data, just in case. You never know if it may be useful in the future. If you're not collecting data yet, start now. Any data you're throwing out, store it somewhere instead. For example, keep track of the products shown to customers that they did *not* purchase. You never know when this information might come in handy or what important insights can be gained from it.

II.   DON'T LET YOUR BUSINESS DEPEND ON THE SUCCESS OF AI (UNLESS YOU CAN AFFORD IT).

Some businesses are built around the promise that AI will do its job. An example is self-driving cars. They rely entirely on the success of novel AI algorithms. But no one knows if these will work. And if the AI fails, the business collapses with it.

Some people keep saying that it's "just a question of time" until a certain algorithm is developed, both for self-driving cars and other problems. I'm skeptical of this statement. If it were a question of time, it would have been done already. With the advent of cloud computing, it is faster than ever to do AI. Even a small company can rent powerful cloud infrastructure at a reasonable price. So, what is holding them back? In reality, no one knows the solution to certain challenging problems. It's not a matter of doing more of the same thing; it is a matter of making a pivotal change in the methodology. Remarkable advances in AI happen because of human ingenuity: devising new, creative ways of solving problems. It is hard to know in advance if that will work out with your problem.

This doesn't mean you shouldn't invest in cutting-edge innovation. But you have to be able to afford the potential losses if you can't find the solution.

Think of how many successful businesses you know were built around an AI product. And by successful I don't mean being funded. I mean generating revenue, paying dividends, exiting. Not so many. Most successful businesses use AI to improve their processes, but they don't rely on the success of these systems to exist.

III.   MEASURE BUSINESS VALUE.

Doing AI is worth it when it brings business value, defined on your own terms. This could be, for example, brand awareness, user experience or, ultimately, dollars. This value has to be measured. An algorithm could have great predictive capabilities but add very little to your bottom line.

The measuring process should be flawless. This is how you catch the sneakiest errors. Managers often blindly trust the results shared by the AI specialists. They think it's all too complicated to dive into so they just trust the figures. But if there is one technical thing you should spend time to understand it's how the added business value is measured. If possible, have an independent team do the assessment. When the same people who do AI measure its value, believe me, funny things can happen.

IV.   BE SHALLOW.

Deep learning has hit the headlines. But it doesn't mean everything has to be *deep*. First of all, deep learning is the name of a technique that works in certain circumstances. It's not about learning more or deeper, in any context. Second, sometimes the simpler solutions are the better fit for the problem at hand and for the business. They provide immense incremental value while remaining easy to understand and manage.

The highest return on investment is in the low-hanging fruit.

Replacing an old-school system with basic machine learning may bring a lot more value than making an existing machine learning setup even fancier.

V.   BURST THE BUBBLE.

It's been years since they first said. "There's only one year left until self-driving cars roam the streets." And it's been centuries since they said all human labor would soon be replaced by technology.

Artificial intelligence is so hyped that it may seem like the world expects your business to do it. I get that all the time from business people: "We *have* to say we're doing AI to get attention from investors."

Now that we've discussed the potential limits of AI, I ask you to do your bit to burst the bubble. Maybe next time someone presents you with a wonderful AI solution, read the small print. Try to see if there's a catch. Maybe next time you present your own work, be realistic and focus on the business value added, not on the AI buzzwords.

I recently stumbled upon an article saying that a music album was "produced *entirely* by AI." If you ever see something like that, don't share it just yet on social media. Dig a bit deeper. I did and discovered that the background instrumentation was done by AI, but the lyrics and the voice—the pieces that made the song sound realistic—were all still human.

CONCLUSION

A couple of years ago, I visited a small museum about cutting-edge technology. It tells the story of London's canals.

The canals in London are part of a complex network of manmade waterways that connect distant parts of Great Britain. You can navigate the canals from the Thames across London and all the way to the north of England.

Back in the day, the canals were used to transport goods on barges. Horses would tow them along the canal by pulling a rope while walking on the path next to the canal. This was a technological wonder at the time because a horse could pull fifty times more weight on a floating barge than on a cart on land. This made the transportation of goods more efficient.

The English went to great lengths to build the canals. There are even portions of them that go through tunnels dug under London two hundred years ago. The horses didn't fit in the tunnels, so the bargemen would lie on their backs on the deck of the boat and push their legs against the ceiling of the tunnel to move the boat along. It could take over an hour to clear a tunnel.

It doesn't sound like cutting-edge technology now, does it?

The London Canal Museum is housed in a building next to a canal that was once owned by an ice merchant. There were no electrical fridges at that time, so if you wanted to preserve food by keeping it cold, you had to purchase ice. This company imported ice from Norway. The ice was brought by sea into the Thames and then transported on barges along the canal. It was then stored in an insulated underground pit, which you can see at the museum. The ice entrepreneur had a fleet of carts to then distribute ice around the city.

Quite an endeavor, just to get some ice.

I'm telling you all this because I found this story quite illuminating. It is easy for us to forget the level of human ingenuity that led us to live the comfortable lives that so many of us live today. We take ice for granted. We take fridges for granted. We take the Internet for granted.

I hope this book has helped you appreciate the complexity of the digital world. A lot goes on to achieve what seems like a simple task. You search for directions on your smartphone and get them almost immediately. But behind every seamless application there are years of work done by techies, who came up with creative solutions and worked hard to optimize them. And doing this effectively required them to abide by a set of engineering principles we've seen repeatedly in this book, including abstraction, reusability, division of labor and collaboration.

I also hope this book has helped you understand, paradoxically, the simplicity of the digital world. It all comes down to ones and zeros and programs that follow strict lists of instructions to the letter. Complex applications are built by combining simple components into more advanced ones and then combining those into larger, more advanced ones still. But even the most complex software is still based on simple principles.

With the advent of the steam engine, the use of canals for commercial freight declined steeply. The steam engine did to canals what the Internet did to fax machines. Some people think that the latest developments in AI are that kind of revolution. Will robots be the next steam engine? I'm a bit skeptical and have shared with you some reasons to temper your expectations of AI. But regardless, there is probably another steam engine on the horizon. What will it be? Who can say?

Thank you for reading Get Tech. If you have time to spare, please let me know your thoughts by leaving a review on the book's Amazon webpage, on Goodreads or elsewhere. I'd appreciate it!

INDEX

A

abstraction 33, 49
A/B testing 188
actionable 76
activation function 196
adding machine 34
ADSL 87
advertising 205
Airbnb 77
airline 117
AJAX 113
algorithm
  complexity 71
  definition 14
  design 70
  heuristic 73
  intractable 73
AlphaGo 209, 211
AlphaGo Zero 210, 211
Amazon Web Services 151
AMD 53
analog 29
and (logic operation) 33
Android 47
anomaly detection 204
API 110, 119, 149
Apple 110, 135

arithmetic in binary 34
artificial intelligence
  always follows instructions 20
  definition 161
  graphics card 41
artificial neural network 193
assembler language 39
asymmetric encryption 130
Australia 88, 155
automatic machine learning 219
availability zone 152
AWS 152

B

back end 109
back-end developer 115
big data 144
binary signal 29
black box 34
black-hat SEO 120
Bletchley Park 129
Bombe 129
browser 123
brute-force attack 127
brute-force optimization 170
bubble in AI 228
business value 186, 227

C

C++ 51, 52
cable 30
cache 38
California 88
CAPTCHA 118
cart 122
cascading stylesheet 105
CCTV 24, 78, 217
certificate 133
character encoding 29
checksum 92
Chrome 101, 123
CIA 135
class 60
classification 163
clock (CPU) 42
cloud computing 151
cluster 45, 145
clustering algorithm 204
CNN 200
coder 49
communication 76
complexity 71
computable problem 13, 18
container 65
control statement 56
control unit 35
convert Fahrenheit to Celsius 19
convolutional neural network 199
cookie 121
cost function 168, 197
COVID-19 23, 175
CPU 35

compilation 52
crawling 119
cross-platform 124
cross-validation 183
CSS 105
cybersecurity 137

D

data
    center 151
    engineer 148, 173
    leakage 183
    protection officer 150
    quality 148
    scientist 173, 196
database 140
dataset 164
DBMS 140, 144
Debian 47
decision tree 168
deep learning 191
    convolutional neural network
        200
    learning from raw data 193
defense 216
delivery of parcels 73
design (software) 66
dial-up 85
difficulty of a problem
    two steps to estimate 24
DigiCert 134
digital 29
digital signature 132, 133
Dijkstra, Edsger 72
diminishing returns
    business value of AI 187
    parallelism 45

disk 20
Django 63
Docker 65
domain name system (DNS) 94
Dropbox 151, 156

E

eavesdropper 125
efficient algorithm 72
Efficient Market Hypothesis 184
electric pressure 28
electronic 28
encryption 126
  assymetric 130
energy function 168
Enigma 128
entrepreneur 76
ephemeral memory 37
epidemics propagation 71
error function 168
error metrics 215
ETL 148
EU 150
European Parliament 217
Excel spreadsheet 23
  business data 139
  interactive 55
  saving 38
executable program 38, 52
explainability 220
exploitation 206, 209
exploration 206, 209
exponential complexity 71
external device 41
external IP address 96

F

Facebook 99, 123, 161
  algorithm to detect face 19
  giving likes 112
Face ID 123, 172
FaceTime 134
facial recognition 202
factorial complexity 71
feature engineering 166
feature extraction 192
features 165
Fedora 47
framework 63
France 188
frequency 43
front end 103
front-end developer 114
full-stack developer 115
function (maths) 194
function (programming) 58

G

gate
  logic 33
  transistor 31
GDPR 150
geographical queries 142
gigahertz
  CPU frequency 43
Gmail 113, 135
GoDaddy 134
Go (game) 203, 209
Google 77, 119, 162
  Cloud Platform (GCP) 152
  Docs 85

Maps 109, 112
Translate 217
GPS 69, 78, 123
gradient descent 171
graphics card 41, 172

H

hacker 135
hard coding 59
hard drive 37
Harry Potter 36
hashing 136
header 104
heat
  melts CPUs 43
heuristic 73
hidden neurons 197
historical data 174
hold-out 180
horizontal scaling 145
HTML 103, 118, 123
HTTP 102, 110
HTTPS 134
human error 213
Hummingbird 121

I

IBM
  Cloud 152
  DB2 140
  playing chess 203
ice merchant 230
iCloud 151
IdenTrust 134

if (programming) 56
image
  as table of numbers 29, 192
  filter 21
  resize 62
ImageNet 164
India 155
inheritance 61
inputs 77
instruction 52
  add 39, 42
  binary 39
  jump 40
  move 40
Intel
  compiler 53
  Core i7 35, 43
  x86 39
interface
  visual 78
  Web API 110
Internet 86
  ADSL, optic-fiber, 4G, Wi-Fi 87
  domain name system 94
  IP address 89
  IPv6 97
  network 88
  network address translation
    (NAT) 97
  node 89
  packet 90
  port number 93
  provider 88
  router 90
  TCP 91
  UDP 94
  VPN 99
interpreted programming lan-

guage 53
interruption (operating system)
    47
intractable problem 73
iOS 47
IP address 89
iPhone 124, 172
IPv6 97
Ireland 154

J

Japan 88, 154
Java 51, 55, 115
JavaScript 107, 115, 118
Java Virtual Machine 55
job interview 74
join (database operation) 143

K

Kaggle 180
key 126

L

label 164, 203
latency 157
learning 162
library 62
light switch 28
limits
    computing 22
    machine learning 213
linear complexity 71
link 105

Linux 47
logic gate 33
login 121
London Canal Museum 230
longest word 145
look-ahead bias 184
loop 57
loss function 168
low level 49

M

Mac 46
MacBook 157
machine code 52
machine learning 22, 162
machine learning engineer 173
macOS 47, 53
Madonna 23
man-in-the-middle attack 133
map 69
margin 169
memory 18
    and CPU 36
    memory-hungry 79
microchip 36
Microsoft
    Azure 152
    SQL Server 140
mobile apps 123
model 166
Morse code 28
motherboard 41
multi-armed bandits 206
multi-core 44

multitasking 46
music produced by AI 228

N

National Security Agency 135
native app 124
needle in a haystack 198
Netflix 98, 144
network 88
network address translation
     (NAT) 97
neural network 193, 195, 210
neuron 195
NLTK 63
node 89
no free lunch 220
notebook 173

O

object-oriented programming 60
object recognition 21, 217
operating system 46
optimization algorithm 170, 197
Oracle 140
organic traffic 120
or (logic operation) 33
outputs 78
overfitting 181

P

packet 90
Panda 121
parallelism

cluster 45
multi-core 44
store-level 43
parameter 167
password 121, 136
pay-as-you-go 152
Penguin 121
Photoshop 36, 62
physical signal 24
pixel 192
policy (reinforcement learning)
     207
polygon 202
port number 93
PostgreSQL 140
PowerPoint 79
predictive performance 180
price optimization 205
prime numbers 131
"print" 51
private key 130
productionizing 173
programmable machine 22
programmer 49
programming
  abstraction 49
  class 60
  control statement (if) 56
  function 58
  loop 57
  object-oriented programming
     60
  "print" 51
  variable 51
programming language
  assembler 39
  C++ 51

Java 51
JavaScript 108
Python 54
Scala 51
public key 130
Python 54, 62, 115
Python Imaging Library 63

Q

Quality software 66
quant 173
quantum computing 48

R

RAM 20
  definition 36
  organization in cells 37
  stores executable program 38
random forest 168
randomness 20
  random.org 21
React 114
read-after-write consistency 140
recalculation (GPS) 69
recommendation 80, 149, 162
redundancy 142, 147
refactoring 66
register 36
regression 163
reinforcement learning 207
relational database 142, 147
resistance 31
resolving IP address 95
resources 79
robots.txt 120

root server 95
router 90
run anywhere 55
running time 73

S

S3 154
Safari 101
satellite images 144, 216
Scala 51
scarcity of IP addresses 96
Scikit-learn 63
scraping 117
screen 29
search engine optimization 120
secondary memory 37
self-driving cars 216, 226
sensible restrictions 202
sentiment 161
server 47
serverless 155
Shopify 67
significance 188
silicon
  material 32, 35
  Silicon Valley 32
Singapore 155
Siri 110
Skyscanner 119
Snowden, Edward 135
social engineering attack 136
software developer 38, 49
Southwest Airlines 118
speech recognition 201
SQL 141, 147

SSL 133
state 14, 18
steam engine 231
stock price 25, 183
straight line 167
supervised learning 203
Switzerland 188
SWMonkey 118

T

table 141
tag (HTML) 103
tape 18, 20, 36
TCP 91
test set 180
text
  encoding 29
  HTML 104
  in interpreted language 53
  program code 50
think computationally 18
tic-tac-toe 208
time-sensitive 80
TLS 133
tornado 153
touchscreen 41
traffic light 15
training a model 172
training data 162, 164, 197
transistor 30, 31
transition 15, 18
translation 25, 161, 211, 217, 222
trial and error 205
Turing, Alan 13, 129
Turing machine 13, 14, 18, 22,
    36, 40

Twitter 56
two-factor authentication 137
type (programming) 51

U

Uber 123
Ubuntu 47
UDP 94
UN 217
underfitting 181
unseen data 179
unsupervised learning 204
U.S. 88, 135
username 135

V

validation of a model 177
validation set 183
value (reinforcement learning)
    207
variable 51
video
  editing 23
  uncompressed 37
visual interface 78
voltage 28, 31
VPN 99, 134

W

water pipes 28
weather forecast 174
Web
  app 102
  architecture 116
  browser 101

cookie 121
crawling 119
definition 101
resource 102
scraping 117
server 102
Welchman, Gordon 129
WhatsApp 134
Wi-Fi 87, 106
Wikipedia 134, 154
Windows 46, 53
wire 30
Wolpert, David 220
WordPress 67
World IPv6 Day 98
Write once, run anywhere 55
WYSIWYG 114

X

xor 33

Y

YouTube 46, 85, 122

Printed in Great Britain
by Amazon